HOW TO STUDY THE BIBLE

A Method for Discovering
Biblical Truth for Yourself

G. Michael Cocoris

© 2010, 2024 by G. Michael Cocoris

All rights reserved. This publication may not be reproduced (in whole or in part, edited, or revised) in any way, form, or means, including, but not limited to electronic, mechanical, photocopying, recording or any kind of storage and retrieval system for sale, except for brief quotations in printed reviews, without the written permission of G. Michael Cocoris, 2016 Euclid #20, Santa Monica, CA 90405, michaelcocoris@gmail.com, or his appointed representatives. Permission is hereby granted, however, for the reproduction of the whole or parts of the whole without changing the content in any way for free distribution, provided all copies contain this copyright notice in its entirety. Permission is also granted to charge for the cost of copying.

Unless otherwise indicated, all Scripture quotations are taken from the New King James Version ®, Copyright © 1979, 1980, 1982 by Thomas Nelson, Inc. Used by permission. All rights reserved.

Cover and interior design by John T. Cocoris

TABLE OF CONTENTS

PREFACE

PART I: PREPARING FOR SPIRITUAL TRUTH   1

Chapter	1	Oh, That I May Know The Truth	3
Chapter	2	The Purpose Of The Bible	9
Chapter	3	The Qualifications For Bible Study	17
Chapter	4	Correct Interpretation	31

PART II: UNDERSTANDING SPIRITUAL TRUTH   65

Chapter	5	Where To Start	67
Chapter	6	Historical Survey	73
Chapter	7	Book Synopsis	91
Chapter	8	Unit Analysis	101
Chapter	9	Textual Exposition	137
Chapter	10	Book Synthesis	155
Chapter	11	Topical Study	177
Chapter	12	Biographical Study	185

PART III: MEDITATING ON SPIRITUAL TRUTH   189

Chapter	13	Meditating On The Evaluation Of Truth	191
Chapter	14	Meditating On The Application Of Truth	201

PART IV: RESPONDING TO SPIRITUAL TRUTH 211

    Chapter 15   The Danger Of Bible Study   213
    Chapter 16   The Appropriate Response   219

PART V: SHARING SPIRITUAL TRUTH 229

    Chapter 17   Begin At Home   231
    Chapter 18   Let The Whole World Know   235

CONCLUSION 239

APPENDIX I: Which Translation Is Best For Bible Study   241

APPENDIX II: An Outline Of Bible History   251

APPENDIX II: The Use And Abuse Of Commentaries   253

BIBLIOGRAPHY 259

ABOUT THE AUTHOR 263

PREFACE

From the moment of my conversion at age eighteen, I have had an unquenchable thirst to know the truth of God's Word. That desire led me to attend Dallas Seminary. In seminary, I had the standard course in hermeneutics. I also took a course on how to study the Bible with Dr. Howard Hendricks. In eight years of academic pursuits, his course was one of my greatest classes.

While a seminary student, I was the pastor of a small Baptist church near Paris, Texas, the First Baptist Church of Pattonville. I no sooner had completed the course on Bible study from Dr. Hendricks than I began to teach it to anyone at the church who would listen. Then, when I graduated in 1966 and moved back to Chattanooga, Tennessee, to commence an itinerant evangelism ministry, I continued teaching individuals and small groups how to study the Bible. I also began to read books on Bible study.

For the next several years, I rethought, revised, and restructured my approach to Bible study several times. I slowly began to formulate a procedure for studying the Scriptures, combining the principles of hermeneutics, the methods of Bible study, and commands from the Scriptures themselves. I also began to apply what I was learning to the New Testament. For thirteen years, I traveled about the country as an itinerant evangelist conducting evangelistic meetings. Behind the scenes, I spent most of my time studying the New Testament. I applied my procedure and made minor adjustments to it.

In 1979, I became the pastor of the Church of the Open Door in Southern California. I preached through biblical books

Preface

alternating between Old and New Testaments. Later, as pastor of The Lindley Church in Tarzana, California, I continued preaching through books of the Bible. Those experiences have given me the opportunity to apply the procedure I had hammered out to every book of the Bible. The process of Bible study that I have practiced for years and now present here will allow you to discover God's truth for yourself.

In her little booklet, *The Joy of Discovery*, Oletta Wald laments that at one point in her life, the treasures of the Bible seemed locked behind closed doors. She had to depend on someone else to open the door. Later, she learned that following a precise step-by-step method of study was like "working a combination lock." When she followed the steps, "the Word opened up to me" (Wald, p. i). The same can happen to you if you follow the proper principles. The procedure presented here is not perfect. No method is. The principles, however, are sound.

I wish to thank Teresa Rogers for proofreading this material. It is sent forth with a prayer that God may use it to provoke believers to search the Scriptures for themselves in a spiritual yet sound and sensible way. May the Lord also be pleased to use this presentation to enlighten and equip believers to be better students of the Scripture and godly saints.

G. Michael Cocoris
Santa Monica, California

PART I

PREPARING FOR SPIRITUAL TRUTH

Chapter 1

OH, THAT I MAY KNOW THE TRUTH

My brother has a proverb; actually, it is a question. He is constantly asking, "How is it really?" When he asks that question, he has in mind life in general and people in particular. Recognizing that what appears to be may not be the way it really is, he has learned to ask, "What is the truth?"

His question has been the cry of my heart for as long as I have known Jesus Christ. How is it really? What is the truth? When praying to God the Father, God the Son said, "Your Word is truth" (Jn. 17:17). If that is correct, and I believe that it is, all I have to do is figure out what God's Word says and I will know the truth. Right?

Well, yes, but there is a problem. The difficulty is that not everyone explains the Bible the same way. When I became a Christian, I quickly learned that there are two, and sometimes more, ways of explaining every passage of Scripture. I discovered that for every doctrine, there are at least two different opinions. Every time I encountered a "problem" passage or a debate over doctrine, I wanted to know, "How is it really? What is the truth? How do I know which interpretation of the Bible is correct?"

Life is filled with dead-ends, decoys, and deceptions. So are ways of handling the Bible! Here are a few detours I have taken.

The Devotional Method

The Method One of the first approaches to the Scripture to which I was introduced was the devotional method. I was urged to read the Bible every day and allow God to speak to me through it. That sounded simple enough. I was to read the Bible and something would "pop off the page" that applied to me personally. When that happened, I had a verse for the day, a word from God, something I needed to apply to my life.

I began to use that approach. As a college student, I was dating a girl whom I really liked, but I wanted to know if it was God's will for me to continue dating her. While reading the book of Proverbs one morning, I came upon the injunction, "forsake her not." I took that as a word from the Lord to me that I should continue dating her.

The Problem Later, I was informed that there was a massive problem with the so-called "devotional" approach to the Bible. Preachers, pastors, and especially professor-types insisted that it was possible to use the devotional method and get a word from the Lord that is not His Word or will at all! The fatal flaw of the devotional method is that it lends itself to making the words of Scripture mean something God never intended to say at all!

When God said, "forsake her not," He did not have my girlfriend in mind. He was talking about wisdom. When He inspired those words and instructed that they be written, He did not intend to apply them to me dating my girlfriend. He was only telling me to make sure I sought wisdom. My application of those words was not a proper use of them; it was an abuse of them.

Those words were true, but I had incorrectly applied them. Then, I discovered another approach.

The Cross Reference Method

The Method Early in my experience as a Christian, I was taught that God was the author of Scripture and, therefore, He was the best interpreter of it. I could allow Him to explain His Word to me by comparing Scripture with Scripture. Does not the Bible say "comparing spiritual things with spiritual" (1 Cor. 2:13)? The answer, of course, is "yes," but the question is, "What does that statement mean?"

Frankly, the phrase "comparing spiritual things with spiritual" is difficult to interpret. In the first place, the word "compare" can mean either "compare" or "interpret." Secondly, in the Greek text, "spiritual things" can either be masculine or neuter. In other words, it can refer to spiritual men or things. Several possible combinations and, therefore, several possible explanations of this statement are possible.

The two most likely possible meanings are: 1) Comparing or interpreting the spiritual message with spiritual words. If this is the correct interpretation, Paul summarizes what he has said thus far in 1 Corinthians 2:6-13. 2) Explaining spiritual truths to spiritually-minded men. If this is correct, Paul has come full circle from the thought expressed in 1 Corinthians 2:6 and introduces what follows.

Everything considered, the latter interpretation seems to best fit all the details of the passage. In short, 1 Corinthians 2:13

says that the apostles spoke words the Holy Spirit gave them and they explained those words to spiritually-minded men. Paul explains that the natural man, the man who does not know Jesus Christ, does not understand the Word of God (1 Cor. 2:14), but spiritually-minded people do (1 Cor. 2:15-16). Then, he tells the Corinthians that he could not speak to them as spiritually mature but as babes in Christ (1 Cor. 3:1).

Thus, 1 Corinthians 2:13 does not teach that the way to study the Bible is by comparing one Scriptural passage to another. It says Paul spoke words the Holy Spirit gave him to spiritually-minded people.

Nevertheless, the method that teaches the way to study the Bible is to compare Scripture with Scripture is not necessarily wrong. Ultimately, that is what needs to be done. Putting truths together, gleaned from several passages, is the topical or theological method of studying the Bible. It is imperative, however, that before several passages are put together, the meaning of each passage is determined independently of all others. Then, and only then, is it legitimate to compare one passage with another passage.

The Danger This approach is often not used properly; it is abused. The abuse is called using a verse as a "proof text." The words of a text are used in a way that the original author did not intend. Consequently, erroneous conclusions are drawn from the text.

It is like the fellow who said, "Lord, speak to me," as he opened his Bible at random and put his finger down. The verse said, "Judas went and hanged himself." He did not like that message; he did not want to hang himself. So, he opened the Bible to another passage and put his finger down on the verse that said, "What you do, do quickly." By taking two statements from two different parts of the Scripture and putting them together, it is conceivable that a person could make the Bible teach "quickly commit suicide!" That is an abusive use of the Scripture.

The Doctrinal Method

The Method Then there is the doctrinal method of Bible study. There are right and wrong uses for this method. The correct application of this approach is to study every passage on a doctrine and conclude what the Bible says about that doctrine. This method is discussed in more detail in the chapter on topical Bible study.

The Wrong Use The wrong use of the doctrinal method is to formulate a doctrine first and then force verses or passages to fit it. Beginning with a verse that sounds like it is teaching that doctrine, this practice coerces other passages to conform.

It is sad to say that I once did that concerning the doctrine of elders. I decided that a church should have a pastor and deacons and that elders in the New Testament were pastors. I forced every passage mentioning elders to fit my preconceived notion, whether or not that was the correct meaning.

This is tortured interpretation. In discussing the forced interpretation of making the seven churches of Revelation the consecutive periods of church history, Hadjiantoniou likens it to the brigand Procrustes of Greek mythology. Victims were placed on a bed. If they were too long, their head was cut off their body. If they were too short, they would have their body pulled at both ends (Hadjiantoniou, p. 13).

Summary: The wrong approach to the Bible produces the wrong conclusions. The misapplication of the devotional method, the cross-reference method, or even the doctrinal method, can lead to a misunderstanding of the Scripture.

Using each of these methods, I have reached incorrect conclusions about what the Word of God teaches about God's will for my life. From bitter experience, I have cried, "How is it really? What is the truth?"

So, what is the proper approach to studying the Scripture? The answer to that question is the subject of what follows, but several preliminary questions must be answered before a method that yields accurate conclusions is described. Why did God write the Bible? Who is qualified to understand the Bible? What determines correct interpretation?

Chapter 2

THE PURPOSE OF THE BIBLE

Why did God write a book? What purpose did He have in mind when He had men write His Word? The Bible contains history, stories, and doctrine. Is God a historian who desires us to know history? Is God a storyteller who delights in telling stories with moral lessons? Is God a theologian who is determined to teach us doctrine? Why did God give people His truth?

For Our Salvation

1 Timothy 3:15 Paul reminded Timothy "that from childhood you have known the Holy Scriptures, which are able to make you wise for salvation through faith which is in Christ Jesus" (2 Tim. 3:15). As soon as they could speak, Jewish children were taught to memorize passages from the Hebrew Scriptures. Paul tells Timothy that his Scripture, our Old Testament, informed him about salvation by faith. At some point in his life, Timothy trusted Christ (2 Tim. 1:5).

Paul says the gospel by which we are saved (1 Cor. 15:2) is that Christ died for our sins according to the Scriptures (1 Cor. 15:3) and rose from the dead according to the Scriptures (1 Cor. 15:4). Again, when Paul speaks of the Scriptures, he is talking about the Old Testament. According to Old Testament, the Messiah would die for our sins (Isa. 53:4-6), not His own (Dan.

9:26) and be raised from the dead (Ps. 16:10). Paul says that is the good news by which we are saved (1 Cor. 15:1-2).

Ephesians 1:13 Paul wrote to the Ephesians, "In Him, you also trusted after you heard the word of truth, the gospel of your salvation; in whom also, having believed, you were sealed with the Holy Spirit of promise" (Eph. 1:13). Paul reminds the Ephesians that they heard the word of truth, which he identifies as the gospel of salvation. The good news about salvation is part of the "truth" in the Scripture. The gospel by which we are saved (1 Cor. 15:2) is that Christ died for our sins (1 Cor. 15:3) and rose from the dead (1 Cor. 15:4). Notice also that salvation is obtained by believing, that is, trusting in Jesus Christ.

God gave us His Word to provide us with truth, by which we can be saved. He gave us truth that enables us to have a relationship with Him.

For Our Sanctification

2 Timothy 3:16 Paul told Timothy, "All Scripture is given by inspiration of God, and is profitable for doctrine, for reproof, for correction, for instruction in righteousness" (2 Tim. 3:16). The Greek word translated "doctrine" means "teaching, instruction." The Scripture is God's instruction manual for how He wants us to believe and behave. The Greek word translated "reproof" means "expose, show fault." The Scripture is profitable for exposing all that is false in doctrine and deportment. The Greek word translated "correction" means "correct, restore." The Scripture shows believers their faults and restores them to the right path. The Greek word translated "instruction" means "training, learning, instruction." It is used of child-training. The Scripture trains believers in righteousness.

In short, God wrote a book so people might become spiritually mature. As believers are exposed to and respond to the spiritual realities in the Word of God, they develop spiritual maturity.

Spiritual maturity consists of being corrected and reproved, that is, removing the vices from our lives. Jesus said you shall know the truth and the truth shall free you (Jn. 8:32). Obviously, knowing the truth is not simply an intellectual exercise. It is having the truth liberate us. From the Scripture, we discover the truths about God, ourselves, and the world. As we face these realities honestly and depend on the Lord for His grace, we experience the liberating power of the Spirit of God from sin, selfishness, and worldliness.

Spiritual maturity is also being taught doctrine and being instructed in righteousness, that is, adding virtues to our lives. Again, as we depend on the Lord for His grace, we experience the power to be what God wants us to be (Heb. 4:16).

Spiritual maturity is the process of replacing vices with virtues. As that becomes the habit of our lives, we develop spiritual maturity.

Titus 1:1 Paul says that he is "an apostle of Jesus Christ according to the faith of God's elect and acknowledgment of the truth which is according to godliness" (Titus 1:1). Part of Paul's purpose is to get people to acknowledge the truth, "which is according to godliness." The Greek word rendered "acknowledge" means "to discern, recognize." Paul's aim was for believers to discern spiritual truths that met the standard of godliness.

John 17:7 Just before He was crucified, Jesus prayed, "Sanctify them by Your truth. Your Word is truth" (Jn. 17:17). Jesus is calling God's Word truth. The Greek word translated "truth" means "truth," that is, "the reality lying at the basis of an appearance; the essence of a matter." It is reality as opposed to mere appearance. It is not just that what God says is true; what He says is truth. His Word contains spiritual reality.

The word translated "sanctify" means "to set apart for God, consecrate, dedicate." Here the idea is to be set apart to the Lord. Believers are set apart to the Lord by the spiritual reality in the Word of God. To say the same thing another way, divine truth is the means (see "by" in Jn. 17:17) of setting believers apart to the Lord.

Jesus taught that the truth of God's Word sets us apart to the Lord (Jn. 17:17). When believers are set apart to the Lord, they become like the Lord (Lk. 6:40). Paul says that there is a truth that leads to godliness (Titus 1:1). The reason God revealed spiritual realities is so that we would grow in godliness.

God gave us His Word to provide us with truth, by which we can be spiritually mature, live Godly lives, and be set apart to the Lord. He gave us truth that enables us to have an intimate relationship with Him.

For Our Service

2 Timothy 3:17 Paul says that all Scripture is inspired and profitable "that the man of God may be complete, thoroughly equipped for every good work" (2 Tim 3:17). The expression "the man of God" refers to all believers. Believers are those who belong to God. The Greek word translated "complete" means "fitted, complete." This thought is repeated again in the expression "thoroughly equipped." In the Greek text, the word translated "thoroughly equipped" is the same root word as "complete" with an added prefix. The addition adds further emphasis to the same thought.

The Scriptures equip believers for every good work (Lk. 6:40; 1 Tim. 5:10; 2 Tim. 2:21; Titus 3:1). "Other writings are profitable for knowledge, for advancement, for amusement, for delight, for wealth" (Plummer). The Scriptures enable us to serve the Lord.

Summary: God gave us His truth in His Word for our salvation, spiritual maturity, and service. In short, God gave us His truth so we can have a relationship with Him.

God's Word contains spiritual realities necessary for people to learn how to have a relationship with the Lord. By believing in His Son Jesus Christ, who died for our sins and rose from the dead, people are saved. When believers know spiritual truth and respond properly to it, they become spiritually mature, becoming more God-like and able to serve the Lord. Therefore, the aim of reading or studying the Bible is to discover those spiritual realities that enable us to have a relationship with the Lord. The object of interacting with the Word of God is to know the Lord, to be like Him and serve Him.

It should also be noted that there is a handling of the Scripture that results in turning people away from the spiritual realities that result in godliness! Paul says believers are not to heed "Jewish fables and commandments of men who turn from the truth" (Titus 1:14).

Based on the genealogies in the Old Testament, some in Paul's day constructed fables (1 Tim. 1:4; Titus 3:9). From this arbitrary and probably allegorical treatment of Old Testament ancestors, these teachers made up commandments of men, which turned believers away from the truth (Titus 1:14). The true ministry is to get believers to acknowledge the truth that produces godliness (Titus 1:1). These useless speculations based on the Old Testament so occupied people's attention that they were turning away from the truth of the Scripture, which would promote godliness in their lives. The study of Scripture is profitable (2 Tim. 3:16); striving over the Scripture is unprofitable (Titus 3:9).

Actually, there is a truth that produces godliness, and there is one that is true but does not. There are historical truths in the Bible, but historical facts do not produce godliness. God is not a historian, a storyteller, or a theologian who wants us to know history, stories with a moral, or even theology. The cry of God's heart is that we know Him and grow in grace and godliness.

All truth is equally valid, but not all truth is equally valuable. A one-dollar bill and a five-dollar bill may be genuine currency, but they are not equally worth. We must distinguish between one-dollar truth and five-dollar truth.

Let me illustrate. Some Bible teachers have argued loud and long about Jonah in the belly of the big fish. They have contended that he died and have listed numerous reasons and irrefutable arguments to prove their point. There is a "truth" concerning Jonah in the belly of the fish. He either died, or he did not die, but frankly, even if what happened could be proven, it still would not necessarily produce godliness. God is interested in teaching us the truth, which is according to godliness, truth that will produce godliness.

So, beware. Bible study can get sidetracked on "truth" that does not sanctify. Do not make the mistake of the scribes. The scribes studied the Law. They were good at understanding the minutiae of the law, but they missed the essential message of what God was saying.

We must remember that Bible study aims to find the kind of truth that enables us to have a relationship with the Lord, grow to be like Him, and serve Him. The Bible was not written so scholars could have a job, nor was it written so that we could be students of it. It was written to produce saints. We must never lose sight of that fact. God's Word is truth, truth that sets us apart to Him. The immediate purpose of Bible study is to find the truth that produces godliness. The ultimate aim is to be godly. In short, do not turn to the truth that does not transform; seek the truth that transforms.

Concerning his book, *Methodical Bible Study*, Traina says, "It should never be forgotten that the ultimate purpose of mechanics and of this manual is that the reader may through their use in studying the Scriptures come to know the real author of the Scriptures, the only true God, and Jesus Christ whom He has sent" (Traina, p. 19).

Chapter 3

THE QUALIFICATIONS FOR BIBLE STUDY

In seminary, I took a course on how to study the Bible. I implemented what I learned. Then, I taught others how to study the Scriptures for themselves. In the process, I learned even more about Bible study. The teacher always learns more than the students do. I also read books on methods of Bible study and found helpful material in them.

After several years of personal study, much reading, and gleaning from others, I began to ask, "What does the Bible say about Bible study?" As I contemplated that question, it dawned on me that the Bible says very little about the method to be used in studying it. I discovered the Bible has more to say about who does the studying than the method of study. Then, one day I came across some old seminary notes of a lecture on this subject given by Dr. Stan Toussaint. Those notes helped put this point in perspective for me.

There are spiritual qualifications for understanding God's Word. Since the purpose of the Word of God is for believers to develop a relationship with the Lord and grow to spiritual maturity, there is a spiritual dimension to understanding the Word of God. The question is, "To whom does God reveal His spiritual truth?"

The Converted

First Corinthians 2:14 Paul declares, "The natural man does not receive the things of the spirit of God for they are foolishness to him nor can he know them because they are spiritually discerned" (1 Cor. 2:14). Jude says the natural man does not possess the Holy Spirit (see Jude 19, where the Greek word translated "natural" in 1 Cor. 2:14 is translated "sensual").

People who do not have the Holy Spirit do not receive the things of the Spirit of God. The word "receive" has the connotation of welcome; it is the usual word for receiving a guest. The things of the Spirit of God are the truths revealed by Him in words. People who do not know God do not welcome or receive God's revealed truth in His Word. Paul goes so far as to say that the Word of God is foolishness to them. The Greek word rendered "foolish" means "dull, insipid, tasteless, stupid."

Furthermore, Paul adds that the unsaved people cannot know the Word of God because it is spiritually discerned. Unsaved people do not have the ability, the power, or the capacity to grasp the Scriptures. Understanding the Word of God requires characteristics that unsaved individuals do not possess. The process is beyond them. The issue is not that they do not or will not; it is that they cannot. Nor is the issue that unsaved people cannot understand the facts of the message of God. It is that they do not draw correct conclusions from them and be changed by them, which is the work of the Holy Spirit. Their evaluation is skewed. The Word of God is to them silly nonsense. Their attitude and aptitudes are not right. Someone has said that a real love letter is ridiculous to everyone but the sender and the recipient.

Shortly after color television was introduced in this country, a viewer wrote a letter to his television station complaining that the pictures were still coming to him in black and white. Accusing the management of deliberately misleading the public, he demanded an apology. As kindly as possible, the broadcast official explained to this disgruntled customer that the color pictures could not be picked up on his ordinary black and white set. The difficulty was not in their transmission but in his receiver. Likewise, the difficulty is not the Word of God but the ability of the unregenerate to receive it.

John 3 Early in His ministry, Jesus went to Jerusalem during the Passover and worked miracles (Jn. 2:23). Nicodemus, a Pharisee and a member of the Sanhedrin, saw the miracles and was deeply moved. He came to Jesus by night and said to Him, "Rabbi, we know you are a teacher come from God for no one can do these signs that you do unless God is with him" (Jn. 3:2). He had seen Jesus working miracles and concluded that those miracles indicated Jesus was from God. His statement implies that he wanted to know more about Jesus, about God, and spiritual things.

Jesus told him, "Most assuredly I say to you, unless one is born again, he cannot see the kingdom of God" (Jn. 3:3). The Greek word translated "see" means "to perceive or discern." Without the new birth, there is no understanding of the kingdom of God, that is, of spiritual things. This statement implies incapability rather than prohibition. Jesus is not saying that such an individual would be arbitrarily barred, but rather that he is inherently incapable, just as a blind man cannot see the sun. Therefore, the new birth is essential to understanding spiritual truth.

Acts 8 In Acts 8, Philip the evangelist came upon the Ethiopian who was reading aloud a portion of Scripture from Isaiah. Philip asked him, "Do you understand what you are reading?" The eunuch replied, "How can I unless someone guides me?" and he invited Philip to come and sit with him (Acts 8:26-31).

If this incident had occurred today, a Christian might have said to him something like, "For you to understand the Bible, you need a modern translation, a paraphrased edition. It's easier to understand." That is not what Philip did. He preached Jesus to him, indicating he did not understand the Scripture because he did not know Jesus Christ (Acts 8:32-39).

For you to understand the truth of God, you must know God. The way to know God is to trust His Son, Jesus Christ, for the gift of eternal life (1 Tim. 1:16). If you have not done so already, tell God that you acknowledge you are a sinner. Tell Him that you believe Jesus died to pay for your sin and rose from the dead and that you now trust Jesus Christ to get you to heaven. When people trust in Jesus Christ and Him alone, plus nothing else, for the gift of eternal life, they come into a relationship with the living God. The Holy Spirit comes into them. He is the one who enlightens believers' minds so they can understand God's truth and be set apart to Him.

I once taught the book of Daniel in a Bible class in downtown Los Angeles. I was explaining the four beasts and ten horns of Daniel 7. After class, a lady came to me and said, "This is the first time I have attended your class, and I must say I did not understand what you said." As I began to explain the four beasts and the ten horns, a friend who brought her interrupted and said, "But do you know that you are going to heaven?" It occurred to me that the lady's problem was not ignorance of prophecy; it was that she did not know Jesus Christ. I immediately explained to her that she needed to trust Jesus Christ for eternal life, which she did. No wonder she did not understand my Bible study. She did not know the Lord!

People who do not know the Lord can understand some of the facts about the Bible but cannot spiritually understand or respond to God. Therefore, it is indispensable that if you are to know the truth of the Word of God, you must know God.

The Clean

Just because people know the Lord does not mean they will automatically understand everything in the Bible. There are other requirements to comprehend all that is in the Scripture. The apostle Peter gives us the next step in the overall process. He says, "Therefore, laying aside all malice, all guile, hypocrisy, envy, and all evil speaking, as newborn babes, desire the pure milk of the Word, that you grow thereby if indeed you have tasted that the Lord is gracious" (1 Pet. 2:1-3). This passage is critical to any approach to understanding the Scripture.

"Laying aside" translates a Greek word used of taking off clothes. Peter lists five sins that must be removed like an old worn-out coat if we are to desire the Word and grow by it. The word "all" divides this list of five sins into three groups or types of sins.

An Attitude The first sin Peter mentions is "malice," which means either wickedness or malice. "All" means "all kinds of," meaning that the first sin in this list is either all kinds of wickedness or all kinds of malice, that is, all ill-will or an attitude of desiring to get even. The context favors the latter meaning. If believers are to love, they must put away all actions and attitudes of ill-will (1 Pet. 1:22).

Actions Guile, hypocrisy, and envy are grouped together by the presence of the second "all." Guile comes from a Greek word that means "bait, craft, deceit." It was used of baiting a fish and denotes deception for personal gain. Hypocrisy means to play a part, pretend. It represents an actor playing a role that hides his true identity. The actions, words, and apparent attitudes of hypocrites conceal their selfish motives. Envy is the feeling of displeasure over someone else's property.

Speech The last category of sins Peter mentions is every kind of evil speaking. The Greek word translated "evil speaking" means "to speak down, to speak against, to slander." Envy usually results in "running down" the other person.

Well-dressed believers do not wear malice, deceit, hypocrisy, envy, or slander. These things are out of style for the child of God. Take off the old rags of the old life by confessing (1 Jn. 1:9) and forsaking (Prov. 28:13) sin.

The Craving

The Command First Peter 2:1-3 consists of a single sentence. Having laid aside sin, believers are to desire the Word of God so that they may grow. The one command in this sentence is "desire." Believers are commanded to desire "the pure milk of the word." The Scripture is referred to as milk because it supplies nourishment. In 1 Corinthians 3:2 and Hebrews 5:12-13, the milk of the Word is for babes; meat is for the mature. Peter does not make that distinction. All believers are to desire the milk, that is, the Word of God.

Believers are to desire the Word of God like newborn babies desires their mother's milk. The image suggests eagerness and intensity. Babies desire milk insistently and regularly.

The purpose of consuming milk is that the believer may grow. As newborn babies cannot grow without milk, spiritual newborns and older believers cannot grow without spiritual milk.

The incentive for consuming milk to grow is that you have already tasted the Lord's goodness and graciousness. The taste of grace and salvation ought to excite the appetite for more of the same. As a pastor friend says, believers need to develop a taste for the Word. Thus, as the babe desires a bottle, believers should desire the Bible.

The Connection In these verses, Peter teaches that there must be cleansing and craving for Scripture. The two are related. Verse 1 contains a participle (laying aside) and verse 2 contains a command (desire). In the Greek text, the action of the participle in verse 1 precedes the action of the verb in verse 2. In other words, there must be the "laying aside" of sin before there will be the "desire" for the Word of God.

D. L. Moody said, "Either sin will keep you from this Book, or this Book will keep you from sin." A dirty life will produce a dusty Bible. If believers are to dig into the Word with a deep desire to know God and His truth, there first must be cleansing.

So, if we are to know God's truth, we must confess, lay aside sin, and earnestly, eagerly desire to know the truth of God and the God of truth.

The Dependent

One might be tempted to conclude that if people know Jesus Christ, are cleansed from sin, and desire to know God's truth, they will successfully find the truth of God. While all of those are prerequisites, they are not the total picture. The Bible teaches that, in the final analysis, God reveals truth to individuals. Therefore, believers must be dependent on the Lord to illuminate their understanding.

God Reveals Truth As Jesus was journeying with the disciples toward Caesarea Philippi, He asked them, "Who do men say that I, the Son of Man, am?" (Mt. 16:13). Their response included answers such as, "Some say John the Baptist, some Elijah, and others Jeremiah, or one of the prophets" (Mt. 16:14). Then, Jesus specifically asked, "But who do you say that I am?" (Mt. 16:15). Impulsively, impetuous Peter immediately answered, "You are the Christ, the Son of the living God" (Mt. 16:16).

Now, who told Peter that? In John 1, the Bible tells us that Andrew, Peter's brother, spent the better part of the day with Jesus Christ and concluded that He was the Messiah. He told Peter, "We have found the Messiah" (Jn. 1:41). Based on that incident, I would assume that his brother Andrew informed him that Jesus was the

Messiah. That, however, is not what Jesus said. In Matthew 16:17, He told Peter, "Blessed are you, Simon Bar-Jonah, for flesh and blood has not revealed this to you, but My Father who is in heaven" (Mt. 16:17). Although Andrew gave Simon the facts, it was God who revealed the truth to him.

The Father reveals spiritual truth to believers through the ministry of the Holy Spirit. The apostle John wrote, "That anointing which you have received from Him abides in you, and you need not that anyone teach you; but as the same anointing teaches you concerning all things that are true, and is not a lie, and just as it taught you, you will abide in Him" (1 Jn. 2:27).

Dependence on the Lord The psalmist cried, "Open my eyes that I may see wondrous things from Your law" (Ps. 119:18). A few verses later, he added, "Make me understand the way of Your precepts; So shall I meditate on Your wondrous works" (Ps. 119:27). The psalmist asked God for an understanding of His Word.

After penning some of the most profound truths in all of the Scripture, Paul fell to his knees and prayed for the Ephesians: "That the God of our Lord, Jesus Christ, the Father of glory, may give to you the spirit of wisdom and revelation in the knowledge of Him, the eyes of your understanding being enlightened; that you may know what is the hope of His calling" (Eph. 1:17-18). Notice that Paul asks God to open the eyes of their understanding that they might know (also Eph. 3:14-19; Col. 1:9-12).

Jesus thanked God the Father that He hid spiritual truth from "the wise and prudent" and revealed it to "babes" (Mt. 11:25). The wise are those who are wise in their own eyes. The babes are God's children. The wise were the intellectually proud. Their preconceived ideas blinded them. Babes are the children of God who are dependent on Him.

Since God the Father, through the ministry of the Holy Spirit, reveals the truth to believers, believers must acknowledge their dependence upon God when they attempt to understand His truth as recorded in the Scriptures. As we acknowledge our dependence on Him in prayer, He gives us an understanding of His Word.

The Spiritually Mature

Even when believers are cleansed and dependent on the Lord, they may not be able to comprehend some of God's truth. In some cases, spiritual maturity is essential.

Hebrews 5 The writer to the Hebrews told Jewish converts that they ought to be teachers, but their spiritual condition was such that they needed to be taught again the first principles of the oracles of God. He says, "For everyone who partakes only of milk is unskillful in the word of righteousness for he is a babe" (Heb. 5:13).

The writer to the Hebrews is not using milk in the same way that Peter used it in 1 Peter 2:1-3. Peter used the metaphor of milk for the Scriptures to illustrate that the Scriptures are nourishing. He commanded all believers to desire the milk of the Word. The writer to the Hebrews, however, makes a distinction between the milk and meat of the Word. He uses the metaphor of milk to refer to the basic truths of the Scripture, whereas meat is the more advanced truth of the Bible. In Hebrews 5:13, he insists that spiritual immaturity will prevent an individual from understanding some of the truths of the Word of God, the meat. The writer goes on to say that solid food belongs to those who are of full age, that is, those who have applied the truths that they have learned so that they will have their senses exercised to discern both good and evil (Heb. 5:14).

First Corinthians 3 Paul had a similar complaint against the believers at Corinth. He said, "I fed you with milk and not with strong food for until now you were not able to receive it and even now you are still not able; for you are still carnal" (1 Cor. 3:2-3a). It was not that they would not; they could not. They were unable to understand some truths.

The conclusion is clear. The spiritually immature cannot understand some of the truths of the Word (see milk in Heb. 5:13); only the spiritually mature can understand the meat of the Word of God (Heb. 5:14).

John 14 We must obey the truth as soon as we understand it. It is then that God reveals Himself and more truth to us. Jesus told the apostles in the upper room, "He who has My commandments and keeps them, it is he who loves Me. And he who loves Me will be loved of My Father, and I will love him and manifest Myself to him" (Jn. 14:21). It is as we obey the Word of God and grow that we will understand more and more of the Scripture and even grow in an intimate relationship with the Lord Himself.

Summary: To understand spiritual truth, believers must deal with their sins, crave God's truth, depend on the Lord, and grow in their relationship with the Lord.

To be transformed by God's truth, believers must be properly related to God. For the truth of God to transform us, we must come to the Scripture with a deep desire to know the Lord and depend on Him to teach us.

There are other qualifications of an interpreter, which will be explained in the next chapter, but the spiritual requirements are foundational. Since the purpose of the Bible is for believers to develop an intimate relationship with the Lord, the spiritual qualifications must be met at all times. Otherwise, the Bible becomes a history book, a storybook, or just a book of doctrine. Who you are as a person is critical to interpreting the Bible. A Chinese proverb says, "If the wrong man uses the right means, the right means works the wrong way" (Kuist, p. 45).

Are you prepared to discover spiritual truth in the Word of God? Here is a list of questions that will help you determine whether you are prepared. Have you trusted Jesus Christ for the gift of eternal life? Are you setting aside sin? Do you earnestly desire to know spiritual truth? Are you dependent upon the Lord to reveal His truth to you? Are you obeying the truth that God has already revealed to you?

It is possible to be highly educated and know Greek, Hebrew, and theology but not know the truth of God or the God of truth. On the other hand, uneducated people who do not know any Greek, Hebrew, church history, or theology know God. They earnestly apply the truth of God as they find it in the Word of God and they grow in their understanding of the Scriptures. They know God and His truth. They are set apart to Him.

In his book *Methodical Bible Study*, Traina calls the kinds of things discussed in this chapter "spiritual sense." He points out that biblical exposition is not a purely mechanical or intellectual process.

He contends that when teachability, sincerity, and intimate knowledge of God are present in a person, that individual has spiritual sense. He says, "The more one possesses these, the more profound will be one's insight into biblical truth. For they have made possible receptivity to God's Spirit, who, having motivated and guided the experience of Scriptural authors, is also their best interpreter." He also says, "In fact, so important is the spiritual factor that one sometimes finds individuals who, though deficient in the skills of interpretation, far surpass in insight those who have had the best training in exegetical procedures" (Traina, pp. 136-37).

According to the Bible, to obtain spiritual truth from the Scriptures, the student of the Scripture must be spiritually prepared. At the same time, there is more involved in arriving at a correct interpretation than just being spiritually prepared. Good and godly believers explain passages differently! Since interpretations often contradict one another, they cannot all be right.

To complicate matters, all expositors claim that they have the mind of the Lord. What determines correct interpretation? Is there some objective way to determine which interpretation God intended?

Chapter 4

CORRECT INTERPRETATION

Being aware of the purpose of the Scriptures and being spiritually prepared are both indispensable to a correct understanding of the Bible, but even spiritually mature believers struggle with understanding some passages. Not even the apostle Peter could easily understand some of the things written by the apostle Paul. He confessed that he found some of the things in Paul's epistles "hard to understand" (2 Pet. 3:15-16).

Wow! Imagine, even after living with the Lord for three years and being filled with the Spirit of God on the day of Pentecost, Peter could not readily understand some Scripture written by the apostle Paul. Peter was certainly converted, cleansed, craving God's truth, and spiritually mature, yet he found some of the things written by the apostle Paul hard to comprehend.

That raises the question, "What determines correct interpretation?" Is there some objective way to discern the meaning the Holy Spirit moved the authors of Scripture to write? The answer is "Yes."

Pardon pointing out the obvious, but the Bible is a book. If God had communicated through music, we would have to understand such things as harmony to comprehend the message. If He had communicated through art, we would have to know such things as color and composition to understand the message. Since God chose to communicate through written material, we have to know things about how written material works. What determines the correct interpretation of written material? What principles can be used as guidelines in the interpretation of written material?

Theories of Interpretation

Interpreting written material is a problem, not just for students of the Scripture but for people in other fields as well. Literary critics debate with each other over how to interpret poems, novels, and plays. Attorneys disagree over the interpretation of contracts and even the Constitution! Expositors and experts differ concerning the explanation of virtually every portion of Scripture. The question is, "How does one interpret written material, including literature, legal documents, or the letters of the apostle Paul?" What determines the correct meaning? What principle determines the validity of an interpretation? Hirsch says in hermeneutic theory (the theories of interpretation), every conceivable norm has been sanctioned (Hirsch Jr., 1976, p. 76). As literary theorists explain, there are three basic possibilities.

The Interpreter One approach claims that the interpreter is the determiner of meaning. The meaning of the text is what it means to the reader. T. S. Eliot even argues that the meaning of written material changes over time (Hirsch Jr., 1967, p. 215).

This approach takes different forms. An elite group can be the only legitimate interpreters of the text. Legal pragmatists "define correct judgment institutionally, as in the majority rule of the Supreme Court" (Hirsch, Jr., 1976, p. 110). For Roman Catholics, the correct interpretation of the Bible is the official explanation of The Roman Catholic Church. Protestants have looked to doctrinal confessions for interpretation (Johnson, p. 11). For some interpreters of the sacred text, the words on the page do not contain the meaning to be communicated. They only establish the basis for a spiritual process, which begins with the words but ultimately transcends them. The process is intuitive. The correct interpretation is determined by inner conviction. Of course, they claim the Holy Spirit gives them insight. Therefore, they are certain that their interpretation is the only valid one.

Thus, for the existentialist in literary criticism, the liberal in political theory, and the neo-orthodox in theology, the interpreter is the determiner of meaning. If that is true, it is impossible to know objectively, for certain, the meaning of a text.

The Text Another method of interpretation insists that the words of the text are the final court of appeal to determine meaning. Historically, this theory is associated with legal interpretation, especially in England (Hirsch Jr., 1976, p. 22). The judge decides based on the principle that a law means exactly what the words of the law say, nothing more or nothing less. Interpretation is determined by linguistic analysis. When rules and canons of construction are applied, the problems of interpretation are solved.

The problem with this approach is that a text may be explained in two different ways. Irony is an illustration (Hirsch, 1976, p. 23).

My wife, Patricia, and her sister, Glenda, are very close. One lives in California and the other in Texas, but they talk a great deal on the phone and look forward every year to Christmas when Glenda visits. One year, just before Christmas, as we were discussing scheduling, I said to Patricia, "And your sister is coming." Patricia replied, "Yes, and I am unhappy about it." I responded, "If I had those words on tape, I could have some fun." Patricia immediately laughed. She and I were aware that what she said (her "text") was the opposite of what she meant. I knew that she was not happy about the length of the visit. In her opinion, it was too short. While the words of a text are essential, the words alone do not determine the meaning of a message!

The Author A third theory of interpretation contends the meaning of the text is the author's intended meaning. The proof of this position is the concept of communication.

The concept of communication is that there is a thought in the mind of one person (author), expressed in the symbols of language and another person (interpreter) interprets those symbols to determine the original thought. Notice the nature of communication is that one person (interpreter) understands the original thought of another. Schodde says, "A person has interpreted the thoughts of another when he has in his own mind a correct reproduction or photograph of the thought as it was conceived in the mind of the original writer or speaker. It is accordingly a purely reproductive process, involving no originality of thought on the part of the interpreter."

According to this view, although the author's intended meaning determines the meaning of written material, the author himself is limited by the norms of language and literature. The nature of written material is that authors desire to communicate a message. They choose language that both they and others understand to convey their meaning. Once that is done, their meaning is limited to the norms of language. Otherwise, understanding is hopeless.

The assumption in communication is that the author is either using language according to a shared meaning or includes enough information to determine the meaning. If an *author* is to communicate with a particular audience, he or she must communicate within the realm of what they share (Johnson, p. 11). As Tan explains, "A *person* is said to 'understand' another when both of them fix the *same meaning* to that which is being spoken or written. This is the basic rule of human communication" (Tan, p. 60, italics added). It is just common sense. People use words with common significance unless they indicate they are departing from the normal, ordinary meaning. Otherwise, there would be no communication!

Communication also assumes that there is only one meaning to what is said or written unless the author indicates otherwise. Tan insists, "Between two persons, the most elementary principle of understanding is that both ascribe the same meaning to that which is being spoken or written. Surely, God would not load His Word with multiple senses and command the prophets to understand. This would be against the rules of fair play. God, in all fairness to the recipients of revelation, could not have intended one thing and then tell His instrumental writers to hear, see, and record other things. It is safe to suppose that God preserved the Scriptural writers from writing anything different from or contrary to what He had in mind to reveal" (Tan, p. 215). Traina insists, "In a given context, every biblical term and statement has one meaning and one meaning only" (Traina, p. 182). In short, as Tan says, "For the speaker to say one thing and mean another is to immediately cut off communication and comprehension" (Tan, p. 60).

Hirsch argues, "To banish the original author as the determiner of meaning is to reject the only compelling normative principle that could lend validity to an interpretation (Hirsch, Jr., 1967, p. 5). In a later book, Hirsch says, "When we simply use an author's words for our purposes without respecting his intention, we transgress what Charles Stevenson in another context called 'the ethics of language,' just as we transgress ethical norms when we use another person merely for our own ends" (Hirsch, Jr., 1976, p. 90). "To treat an author's words merely as grist for one's own mill is ethically analogous to using another man merely for one's own purposes" (Hirsch, Jr., 1976, p. 91). Hirsch's answer to all the critics of this position is, "Would they want others to disregard their intended meaning of their writings" (Hirsch, Jr., 1976, p. 91)?

Therefore, the correct interpretation of written material is the author's intended meaning. As Johnson says, "The goal of interpretation is to know the author's intended meaning as expressed in what is said or what is written" (Johnson, p. 15).

In *Through the Looking Glass*, Lewis Carroll has Humpty Dumpty say, "When I use a word, it means just what I choose it to mean—neither more nor less!" Even Humpty Dumpty understood that meaning is the intended meaning of the author.

How does all of this apply to the Bible? To complicate matters, on the one hand, the Bible is like any other book; yet, on the other hand, it is not like any other book. These two seemingly contradictory truths make the Bible a unique book. The Bible is like any other book in that human authors wrote it. The individuality of the various human authors of Scripture is apparent. John has a different style than James and Paul has a different style than Peter. At the same time, the Bible is not like any other book. It is the only book in the world written by God (2 Tim. 3:16)!

Describing the Old Testament Scriptures, Peter says, "Knowing this first, that no prophecy of Scripture is of any private interpretation, for prophecy never came by the will of man, but holy men of God spoke as they were moved by the Holy Spirit" (2 Pet. 1:20-21). The Scriptures were not self-inspired; they were Spirit-inspired. The Greek word rendered "moved" was used of a ship being carried along by the wind (Acts 29:15, 17). The Holy Spirit moved the authors of Scripture in the direction He wished so that what they wrote was the Word of God.

Thus, the correct interpretation of the Bible is the meaning intended by the Author/author. Johnson says, "The Bible adds a factor that no human literature contains: God spoke through human prophets and through the words written by human authors. These human authors were responsible for the form of the text. Yet, the Author, not the authors, ultimately determined what was to be communicated" (Johnson, p. 26).

Conservative biblical scholars have always taken the author of Scripture seriously. They talk about "historical/grammatical hermeneutics," which Terry defines as the interpretation of the author's "language as is required by the laws of grammar and facts of history" (Terry, p. 101). The purpose of the historical/grammatical interpretation is to "discern what meaning the author intended to communicate to his readers" (Longman III, p. 28).

Therefore, in the words of Johnson, "The ultimate goal (of interpretation) is the single, unified meaning originating with

with the divine Author, as expressed by the human authors" (Johnson, p. 51). When it comes to interpreting the Constitution of the United States, Anthony Scalia, the Supreme Court justice, calls himself an originalist. He interprets the Constitution as the original authors intended.

General Principles of Interpretation

So, since the correct interpretation of written material is the intended meaning of the author and, in the case of the Bible, the meaning intended by the Author/author. What are the principles of interpretation?

The technical term for the study of the interpretation of the Bible is hermeneutics. The dictionary definition of "hermeneutics" is "the science of interpretation," especially of the Bible. In Greek mythology, Hermes (Mercury in Roman mythology) was the messenger of the gods. He is generally pictured with winged shoes, a hat, and a caduceus (a caduceus is a winged staff with two serpents twisted about it). He is supposed to have invented language as a medium of interpretation of a message of the gods.

The academic discipline of hermeneutics is divided into general hermeneutics and special hermeneutics. General hermeneutics includes broad, general principles of interpretation. Special hermeneutics deals with the interpretation of various types of literature. The principles of general hermeneutics can be summarized as follows.

Inspiration All Scripture is given by inspiration of God (2 Tim. 3:16). The Greek word translated "inspiration" means

"God-breathed, inspired by God." Paul does not say that the authors of Scripture were inspired. He says the Scriptures themselves are inspired. That does not mean that the inspiration of the Scriptures was mechanical. The different personalities of the authors of Scripture are apparent. The Holy Spirit (2 Pet. 1:21) worked through the human authors of Scripture, and the result was that their words were the very words God intended to be employed to express His truths. Since the object of correct interpretation is to determine the author's intent and God is the Author of the Bible, the ultimate aim of the interpretation of the Bible is to determine what God intended to communicate.

Accommodation God used human languages, not a special heavenly language, to communicate His message and, in doing so, accommodated Himself to the laws of language and literature. Therefore, God's inspired Word must be interpreted according to the regular rules of understanding the languages and the types of literature He used.

If I were to go to a country where people spoke Spanish, I could either speak English and demand that anyone who communicated with me learn English, or I could learn Spanish and use their language to communicate with them. If I chose to learn Spanish, I would accommodate myself to them. I would also use words with the definitions that those words had to them. One of the laws of language is that there is a shared and single meaning of the words used.

Analogy of Faith Since God inspires all Scripture, there is unity in what the Bible teaches. Every interpretation must be in harmony with the uniform teaching of Scripture (Tan, p. 110). There is one and only one system of doctrine taught in the Bible (Ramm, p. 90). There are no contradictions in the Scripture (Ramm, p. 89). Any appearance of self-contradiction is an illusion.

Progressive Revelation The Bible was not dropped from heaven all at one time. It was written over many centuries. Furthermore, it is evident that over these many centuries, there was a progression in the information given on many subjects. Therefore, the Bible is to be interpreted in view of the fact that it progressively reveals truths.

Revelation in the Bible progresses from the partial to the complete, from the temporary to the final. The Old Testament is a partial revelation (Col. 1:26); with the New Testament, God's revelation is complete in His Son (Heb. 1:1-2; Jude 3). The Old Testament is a temporary revelation (Rom. 6:14; Gal. 3:23-25; 2 Cor. 3:5-11), while the New Testament is now final (Jude 3; Rev. 22:18-19). Simply put, "The Old Testament is old, and the New Testament is new" (Traina, p. 157).

That does not mean that the Old Testament is worthless. While it is true that believers today are not under the law (Rom. 6:14), the Old Testament was written for our learning (Rom. 15:4). All Scripture is profitable (2 Tim. 3:16). Traina illustrates this truth by saying, "For even copies of old newspapers are kept because they contribute much to an understanding of that which is happening today. The same function is performed by the Old Testament in relationship to the New Testament" (Traina, p. 157).

Illumination In the final analysis, God must enlighten the minds of believers so that they can understand His Word (Ps. 119:18; Eph. 1:18).

Application Although God wrote His Word to specific people in history, His intent is to apply its spiritual truth to all believers of all ages. Although written 1500 years earlier to the Jews, Paul says that the historical events recorded in Exodus and Numbers were written for us, that is, for Gentile believers (1 Cor. 10:11). When the Pharisees complained that His disciples were picking grain on the Sabbath, Jesus replied, "Have you not read what David did" (Mt 12:2). Jesus assumed what was written a thousand years earlier, applied to His day. First Peter was originally addressed to believers who were sojourners in the Roman providence of Asia Minor. Yet the book was intended for all believers of all time. Peter concludes the book by saying, "Peace to you all who are in Christ Jesus" (1 Pet. 5:14). In Revelation chapters 2-3, seven specific local churches received seven inspired letters, but those letters were also intended for all churches. At the end of each letter, Jesus says, "He who has an ear, let him hear what the Spirit says to the churches" (Rev. 2:7; 2:11, 2:17, 2:29; 3:6, 3:13, 3:22). Notices, each letter is addressed to an individual church, yet Jesus says that the Spirit was speaking to the churches (plural). There is a universal truth in the messages to particular local congregations.

Also, it is generally agreed that there is one meaning (Ramm, p. 87), but there are many applications (Ramm, p. 88).

All of these general principles are accurate, but they are too general to be of any practical assistance in interpreting a particular passage of Scripture. Hirsch points out that the range of application of the rules of interpretation is limited (Hirsch Jr., 1967, p. 200). He says, "It may be set down as a general rule of interpretation that there are no interpretive rules which are at once general and practical" (Hirsch Jr., 1967, p. 202).

The Specific Principle of Interpretation

If general principles of interpretation are impractical, are there specific principles that determine the Author/author's intended meaning? Yes.

Context One of the first and foremost principles of interpretation is context. A text, apart from the context, is a pretext. In the Bible, there is an immediate context (the paragraph as well as the surrounding paragraphs), the basic context (the book), and the ultimate context (the Testament and, beyond that, the Bible).

1. Context determines the meaning of words. A word can have many meanings. A dictionary lists all the possible meanings. For example, the word "ball" is meaningless if it appears alone. It could be a ping-pong ball, golf ball, tennis ball, baseball, softball, basketball, football, dance, or a good time. "Ball" can be used literally (football) or figuratively (a good time). Context determines the meaning of the word "ball."

Likewise, the word "trunk" can mean several entirely different things, such as back in of the car, the front end of an elephant, a large container for storing possessions, the thick main stem of the tree from which branches grow, the main part of a person's body, not including the head, arms, or legs.

Without additional information, the meaning a word in a sentence is uncertian. Context determines the meaning of words.

2. Context determines the meaning of a sentence. A sentence can have several different meanings. Two people were walking down the street. One said to the other, "You're beautiful." What does that mean? Because that sentence can have several interpretations (meanings),

Correct Interpretation

more information (context) is needed to determine which meaning was intended by the speaker.

If the speaker was the captain of the football team talking to the head of the cheerleading squad he was dating, he meant she was physically beautiful. If, however, the speaker was an 80-year-old lady talking to another 80-year-old lady, both having just come from a soup kitchen where they were helping to feed homeless people, the speaker meant her friend was a beautiful person inside; she was kindhearted. If the speaker was a 20-year-old man talking to another 20-year-old man who had just said something unkind, the speaker meant the exact opposite of beautiful, namely, that what you said was ugly.

Without additional information, a sentence can have several different meanings. Context determines the meaning of a sentence.

Relationships Another major principle of interpretation is relationships. That is true of words within a sentence, sentences within a paragraph, paragraphs within a group of paragraphs (sections), sections within a group of sections (divisions), and divisions within a group of divisions (a book). Some of these will be discussed later, but consider the following examples.

1. Relationships determine meaning within a paragraph. A paragraph contains more than one sentence. When more than one sentence is present, the issue becomes the relationship between the various sentences. Some sentences are "coordinate" with each other, and some are "subordinate" to another sentence.

For example, a wife emailed her husband while he was at work. The email said, "Please stop by the grocery store on your way home. Buy a gallon of milk. Be sure to get the brand I like. We also need a dozen eggs. Pick up your shirts at the cleaners.

Stop by the post office to buy a roll of stamps. We need more stamps to send invitations to our daughter's birthday party. That paragraph could be analyzed as follows.

> Please stop by the grocery store on your way home.
> Buy a gallon of milk.
> Be sure to get the brand I like.
> We also need a dozen eggs.
> Pick up your shirts at the cleaners.
> Stop by the post office to buy a roll of stamps.
> We need more stamps to send invitations to our daughter's birthday party.

In other words, some ideas (sentences) in that paragraph are "coordinate" (parallel) to each other. The sentence "Stop by the grocery store" is "coordinate" (parallel) with the sentence "Pick up his shirts at the cleaners," and the sentence "Stop by the post office to buy a roll of stamps" is "coordinate" (parallel) with the sentence "Stop by the grocery store. In other words, three sentences in that paragraph are "coordinate" (parallel) to each other.

Some of the ideas (sentences) in that paragraph are "subordinate" to another idea (sentence) in that paragraph. For example, "Buy a gallon of milk" and "We need a dozen eggs" or subordinate to "Stop by the grocery store." Also, "Be sure to get the brand I like" is a "subdivision" to "Buy a gallon of milk." These are "subordinate" ideas.

All of the ideas (sentences) in that paragraph are related to an overall "big idea" that is not necessarily stated. In this case, it would be, "On your way home, run these errands."

2. Relationships determine meaning beyond the paragraph. When a document contains more than one paragraph, each paragraph has a "big idea" and all the paragraphs put together have an overall, all-encompassing "big idea." Read Psalm 19.

Stop. Do not read anything else written here until you have read Psalm 19.

Now, let's analyze Psalm 19. Twice, the author abruptly changes subjects. So, Psalm 19 clearly consists of three paragraphs. Each of these paragraphs has an "idea:" In the first paragraph, the psalmist says the heavens declare the glory of God (Ps. 19:1-6). Then, he abruptly changes subjects. In the second paragraph, the psalmist says, in essence, the Word of God reveals the will of God (Ps. 19:7-11). After that, he abruptly changes the subject again! In the third paragraph, the psalmist expresses a desire to be pleasing to the Lord (Ps. 19:12-14).

Although this psalm has abrupt changes, it is a unit. Therefore, the three paragraphs are related to each other. The all-inclusive "big idea" of all three paragraphs put together is "When you see God's revelation of His glory in the world and His will in His Word, your response should be for God to cleanse you, keep you from sin, and give you the strength for your words and thoughts to be acceptable." That could be shortened to, "When you see the glory of God in the world and the will of God in the Word, we should have the desire to please God." The overall "big idea" of the entire psalm is not stated, but the sum of everything in each paragraph can be stated in a single sentence.

In the books of the Bible, groups of paragraphs make up

sections, and groups of sections make up divisions. Each of these sections and divisions has a "big idea."

3. Relationships determine the message of the whole book. The book has one overall, all-encompassing, single "big idea." The book of Exodus has three main divisions: God redeemed Israel from Egypt (Ex. 1:1-18:27), God made a covenant with Israel (Ex. 19:1-24:18), and God established the Tabernacle (Ex. 25:1-40:38). Putting those three divisions together, the all-encompassing "big idea" of the book of Exodus is that God not only redeemed Israel and gave them His Law, He dwelt among them. The point is that the purpose of redemption is for God to give us His Word and His presence.

Selection Another major principle of interpretation is selection. Traina observes, "Selectivity is inherent in all literature and, in fact, in all art" (Traina, p. 85). The famous author Goethe states, "The artist is known by selection." Traina also says, "*Purposive selectivity characterizes the Bible*. In other words, biblical authors had definite purposes, which motivated the writing and they chose their materials and utilized them in such a way so as best to accomplish the purposes" (Traina, p. 59, italics his). Types of material include biographical material (people; see Genesis), historical material (events; see Numbers), logical material (ideas; see Romans), etc. (see Traina, pp. 55-56).

1. Selectivity involves what authors *include* and *exclude* (Traina, p. 59). Omission has been called "the one art of literature" (Stevenson quoted by Traina, p. 75). When Paul wrote Galatians, he followed the format of an ancient letter, which included a thanksgiving, but in Galatians, he did not include the thanksgiving feature. His exclusion of this standard part of a letter is significant. He

was not thankful for believers departing so quickly from the gospel.

2. Selectivity involves the *amount* of material an author chooses to include. Authors devote the most material to the most significant portion of their work. Traina calls this the law of proportion, which he says "involves the principle that an author devotes the greatest quantity of material proportionally to what he feels is most significant and most helpful in conveying his message" (Traina, p. 61). He also says that the sheer weight of a series of similar events or ideas impresses facts on the minds of readers (Traina, p. 61).

Traina suggests asking a series of questions. "Why did the author include this particular event or idea? Why is it where it is? What does it contribute to the whole in view of its relation to the surrounding events or ideas" (Traina, p. 62)?

Arrangement Authors arrange their selected material. It is the arrangement that makes written material literature. What is literature? Literature is written material, but not all written material is literature. A grocery list and a legal brief are written, but neither would be considered literature. What, then, distinguishes a piece of written material as literature?

The subject matter of all literature is human experience. A written, scientific description of inanimate things is not literary. "Literature is a specially privileged subject matter which tells us more about man in his depth and breadth than any other discipline" (Hirsch, 1967, p. 148). Even poems about trees deal with human experience. Thus, Joyce writes, "I think that I shall never see a poem as lovely as a tree." Not all written material about human experience, however, is literature. Psychology books are not literature.

Literature is not only about human experience; it is the artistic arrangement written about human experience. Literature has structure. Structure permeates literature. In that sense, the Bible is literature.

Human authors of legendary literary works have testified that producing literature is long, hard work. In his commentary on Matthew, Barclay says, "In *The Art of Poetry*, Horace advises Piso, when he has written something, to keep it beside him for nine years before he publishes it. He tells how a pupil used to take exercises to Quintilius, the famous critic. Quintilius would say, 'Scratch it out; the work has been badly turned; send it back to the fire and the anvil.' *Virgil's Aeneid* occupied the last ten years of Virgil's life, and, as he was dying, he would have destroyed it because he thought it so imperfect if his friends had not stopped him. Plato's *Republic* begins with a simple sentence: "I went down to the Piraeus yesterday with Glaucon, the son of Ariston, that I might offer up prayer to the goddess. On Plato's own manuscript, in his own handwriting, there were no fewer than thirteen different versions of that opening sentence. The master writer had labored at arrangement after arrangement so that he might get the cadences exactly right. Thomas Gray's *Elegy written in a Country Churchyard* is one of the immortal poems. It was begun in the summer of 1742; it was finally privately circulated on 12th June 1750. Its lapidary perfection had taken eight years to produce. No one ever arrived at a masterpiece by a short-cut" (Barclay, *Matthew*, vol. I, p. 283-284).

Whether produced by tedious labor or with the aid of the Holy Spirit, great literature contains *artistic arrangement*. The structure of written material may be divided into grammatical structure and literary structure.

1. Grammatical structure is within the sentence. The technical word for structure within a sentence is syntax. The dictionary definition of "syntax" is "the arrangement of words in a sentence to show the *relationship* (italics added) to each other." Grammatical relationships include 1) the *relationship* between the subject and the verb, 2) the relationship between the verb and the object, 3) the relationship between the modifiers and the modified, 4) the relationship between the preposition and its object, 5) the relationship between the pronoun to its antecedent, and 6) the relationship of coordinate clauses to each other in compound sentences and the relationship of dependent clauses in complex sentences.

Each of these relationships can have meaningful significance, but most of the time, a detailed analysis of these relationships is not necessary. As Traina says, "One may observe the fact that 'Jesus took with him Peter, James, and John' without being conscious that 'Jesus' is the subject of the clause, that the verb is 'took,' and that the prepositional phrase 'with him' modifies the verb, and that 'Peter, James, and John' are the direct objects of the verb connected to each other by the conjunction 'and'" (Traina, p. 49). In fact, he says, "One of the weaknesses of the traditional approach to exegesis has been its emphasis on grammatical relations at the expense of the sensitivity to literary structure" (Traina, p. 84).

2. Literary structure includes the *relationship* between sentences, paragraphs, segments, subsections, sections, divisions, and the book. A paragraph is a group of sentences constituting a unit of thought (Traina, p. 37). According to Traina, a segment is a

group of paragraphs that constitute a unit of thought, a subsection is a group of segments that constitute a unit of thought, and a section is a group of subsections (or segments) that constitute a unit of thought. He goes on to say that a division is a group of sections that constitute a unit of thought and a book is a group of divisions that constitute a unit of thought (Traina, p. 37).

Notice a sentence, a paragraph, a segment, a subsection, a section, a division, and a book all constitute a unit of thought. By definition, a sentence is a complete thought. Paragraphs contain a series of sentences put together to form another thought. To determine the thought of the paragraph as a whole, the interpreter has to trace the development of the thought through the paragraph. To ascertain the thought of a subsection, section, division, or book, the relationship between the units in each of these must be analyzed.

Authors utilize both explicit and implicit structures. Explicit structure is immediately apparent to the trained observer. For example, the author says, "therefore," indicating a cause-and-effect relationship in the construction of the material. Implicit structure is less obvious, such as an implied contrast between two individuals or ideas (Traina, p. 38).

Since structure is such a fundamental part of authors communicating their message and accomplishing their purpose, it is vitally important that interpreters become aware of structure. Traina urges readers to become "structure-conscious" to comprehend the message of the author (Traina, p. 37). So remember, the critical issue in structure is relationships. After determining the structural units, ask, "How are these units related to each other? What function does each unit perform in relation to the other units?" (see Traina, p. 65).

One other word: there are numerous types of literature. A narrative is a story, a unified sequence of events. The storyteller selects material and proportionately arranges it to make a point. Stories appeal to the imagination. The historical books in the Old Testament and the Gospels in the New Testament are of this type. Poetry is a highly structured form of writing that frequently utilizes figurative language. It appeals to the emotions. In the Bible, the Psalms, as well as large portions of the prophets, are poetry. Discourse or prose presents ideas in a logical form. Ideas are developed. There is a logical development of thought, a train of thought. "This type of literature appeals primarily to the intellect" (Traina, p. 69). Biblical examples include the prophetic sermons in the Old Testament, the discourses of Jesus, and the epistles of the New Testament. These and other types of literature are described in more detail in the chapter on Unit Analysis.

Literary forms are called "literary genres." The word genre simply means "type, class." Ramm says, "An appreciation of literary genre is indisputable for the understanding of Scripture because so much of Scripture (in a sense all of Scripture) is expressed in some kind of literary genre" (Ramm, p. 142). Later, Ramm says that no book of the Bible can be intelligently interpreted without first noting its literary genre (Ramm, pp. 146-147).

To sum up, authors communicate a message (a truth summarized in a sentence) by selecting material (selection) and arranging it (structure) into various forms that constitute types of literature.

The Gospel of John is a biblical illustration. In his commentary on the Gospel of John, Westcott says John is guided in the selection, arrangement, and treatment of his material by his desire to fulfill his purpose (Westcott, p. xlii). John's subject is Jesus Christ, the Son of God (Jn. 20:31). John selected stories, such as the conversation with Nicodemus, and arranged them chronologically to demonstrate that Jesus is the Christ, the Son of God. His purpose was to get his readers to believe in Jesus Christ for eternal life.

The Process of Interpretation

The job of the interpreter is to determine the author's intended meaning. To do that, the interpreter has to reconstruct what was in the author's mind. Interpreters need to stand in the author's shoes and adopt his or her mentality and particular point of view (Traina, p. 152). The process is complex and sometimes difficult. The interpreter searches for evidence in the author's world, culture, choice of literature, logic, attitude, language, etc. (see Hirsch, 1967, p. 242).

Most of this information comes from what the author has written. In the case of the Bible, God communicated spiritual truth (ideas) to a specific situation (history) through human authors in various literary forms (literature) in several different languages (languages). In other words, the historical situation, type of literature, and meaning of the original language provide clues to reconstructing the ideas in the mind of the author/author of Scripture.

To say the same thing another way, the Bible consists of form and substance. The form is a statement, a story, a poem, a parable, etc. (literature) written years ago to a specific situation (history) in another language (language). The substance is the spiritual truth, the thesis, the ideas, the concept, the principle, the message. The form is the vehicle to communicate the substance. The form (statements, stories, poems, etc.) is the wrapping. The substance (spiritual truth) is what is inside. The cow is the form; the steak is the substance.

Interpreters must deal with the form to get to the substance. Kuist emphatically declares, "Form is the key which unlocks the door of content and discloses the essence of the subject matter" (Kuist, p. 92). Jensen concurs, "A Christian who studies a book of the Bible with serious intentions must learn its facts by way of its form" (Jensen, p. 29).

The interpreter's task is to unwrap the package, peel away the form, get past the form, and find the substance. The student must crawl through the history, literature, and language to understand the spiritual truth. The substance (spiritual truth) sanctifies us. The Spirit of Truth uses the Word of Truth to transform believers (Rom. 12:2; 2 Cor. 3:18).

When the children of Israel returned to the land after the exile, they faced the same situation we experience with the Scripture today. Therefore, Ezra and others "helped the people understand the Law" (Neh. 8:7). What did they do? "They read distinctly from the book, in the Law of God; and they gave the sense, and helped them to understand the reading" (Neh. 8:8).

Notice the process. First, they read distinctly. This probably means they translated the Hebrew text of Moses. Later in the book of Nehemiah, it says, "Half of their children spoke the language of Ashdod, and could not speak the language of Judah, but spoke according to the language of one or the other people" (Neh. 13:24). In other words, some from Babylon spoke Aramaic, so when Ezra read, he translated Hebrew into Aramaic.

They gave the "sense," a Hebrew word that means "to have insight, to comprehend." They help people understand. They exposed, explained, expounded the meaning of the text so that people got the sense and insight into what was being read; the people understood.

They helped them understand. Ezra was reading something written by Moses about 1400 BC. He and the people to whom he was reading lived about 446 BC. Moses had written five books at a different time and in a different language. In other words, they heard a Hebrew Bible with Babylonian ears. Thus, they had to understand the message given through history (1000 years before), literature (law), and language (Hebrew).

Today, we hear a Hebrew/Greek Bible with English/American ears. If we are to understand the Scripture, we, like the people in Nehemiah 8, must understand its message through history, literature, and language.

The Historical Context God has revealed His glory (Ps. 19:1) and deity (see the word "Godhead" in Rom. 1:20) to all through creation. On isolated occasions, He has revealed Himself and His message directly to individuals through speech, visions, and dreams (Heb. 1:1). He has also chosen to reveal Himself and His will in His Word through various historical situations. In other words, God revealed Himself and His eternal truth to a select group of people in time. They recorded it for the benefit of the rest of us. Paul says, "All Scripture is given by inspiration of God, and is profitable for doctrine, for reproof, for correction, for instruction in righteousness" (2 Tim. 3:16).

Moses wrote about 1446 BC. (It is possible and probable that Job was written before Moses.) This written record was "once for all delivered to the saints" (Jude 3) through the apostles by AD 95. Hence, it is generally said that the Bible was written over a period of fifteen hundred years. (If Job was written during the Period of the Patriarchs, the period is more like two thousand years.) That is a lot of history. God used hundreds of people, events, and historical situations to reveal His eternal truth.

Thus, if we are to understand God's eternal truth, we must begin with the historical situation. Students of text written in the past are historians (Hirsch Jr., 1967, p. 138).

The Literary Context The Bible contains many different types of literary forms, literary genres. The major types of literature in the Bible are narrative, poetry, proverb, prophecy, parable, and epistle. By virtue of the fact that God chose the medium of literature to communicate, He is abiding by the norms that govern each of these literary forms. As Hirsch points out, "If I write a novel, then what I write must partake of the nature and the implicit aims of a novel" (Hirsch, 1967, p. 151).

Therefore, for us to understand what God is communicating to us in His Word, we must understand these types of literature and the principles that "regulate" them. Longman observes that the correct interpretation of the Song of Solomon depends on accurately identifying the literary genre. If it is an allegory, it describes the relationship between a believer and the Lord. If it is a poem, it is extolling the love between a husband and wife (Longman III, p. 27).

The Linguistic Context The message God recorded in a historical situation using various types of literature is written in words, that is, language. In order for us to understand the message of God, we need to know the meaning of words and the significance of the way they are arranged. Yes, we need to know a bit about grammar. The Old Testament was written in Hebrew and Aramaic and the New Testament was written in Greek. The meaning of a word or phrase in the original language is the correct meaning. An accurate translation will communicate those meanings. (In my opinion, The New King James Version is the most accurate translation, especially for Bible study. I explain why in Appendix 1.)

The Message Context To a specific group of people, in a particular historical situation, using a type of literature, God delivered spiritual truth, His message. The message, the author's intended meaning, is in the form of a thought, an idea. So, the correct interpretation is to understand the author's idea. It is reproducing the idea that is in the writer's mind. If the nature of the author's intended meaning is an idea, what does an idea look like? An idea is more than a single word. An idea consists of a subject (topic) and something said about that subject. The something said about a subject (the completion of the subject) is called a complement (Haddon Robinson) or an assertion (Don Sunukjian). The combination of a subject and assertion is an idea, "a complete thought" (a message).

"Car" is not an idea. "Car" is a subject, which is the first part of an idea, but something needs to be added for the word "car" to be an "idea." An idea would be, "My car is for sale." The word "car" by itself is a fragment; it is not a complete thought. Anything less is a meaningless fragment. So, well-written material consists of an idea, a subject and an assertion.

1. Subject. Most subjects are too large to cover in one article or book. So, writers have to narrow their subject. The apostle John chose to write about Jesus but knew he could write about everything concerning Jesus. He says if everything Jesus did were written, "I suppose that even the world itself could not contain the books that would be written" (Jn. 21:25). John restricted his subject to some of the things Jesus said and did in Jerusalem. John's subject is Jesus. His narrow subject is Jesus as the Christ, the Son of God (Jn. 20:31).

2. Assertion. Writers have something to say about their narrowed subject. What John has to say about Jesus as the Christ, the Son of God, has to do with eternal life (Jn. 20:31).

3. Message. The combination of a narrowed subject and what is said about that subject in a well-written book can be (should be) stated in a single sentence. That single sentence is the author's message. John's message is that those who believe Jesus is the Christ, the Son of God have eternal life (Jn. 20:31; 3:36).

The Confirmation of the Correct Interpretation

As people grapple with the historical situation, the type of literature, and the meaning of language to obtain the message in the mind of the Author/author of Scripture, there is a process that naturally occurs (see E. D. Hirsch, Jr., *Validity in Interpretation*).

Interpreters either read the written material with a preconceived notion of its meaning or develop a preliminary concept of its meaning as they read it. This notion or concept of the whole will determine their understanding of details, which is why interpreters differ and disagree. A preconceived notion or a preliminary concept is an interpretive hypothesis, which tends to be self-confirming (Hirsch, 1967, p. 166). This original perception is a working hypothesis that needs to be verified by data in the text.

There is an interdependency of the whole and the parts. The whole can only be understood through its parts. The parts can only be understood through the whole. If the parts do not explain the original idea of the whole, that idea must be discarded or revised. Often, interpreters begin with a vague or broader idea and, in the course of interpretation, merely narrow it down or make it more explicit. The process of interpretation is the process of trial and error, revision and refinement until the interpreter arrives at an overall idea that explains all the details and an explanation of all the details that fit the whole.

In his famous "Essay on Composition," John Ruskin defines composition as "literally and simply, putting several things together, so as to make one thing out of them." That one thing is the key to interpretation. When that one thing explains the details (and the details fit the one thing), the interpreter understands the intended meaning of the Author/author of Scripture.

Thus, a passage of Scripture has a subject, a message, material selected to develop the message (selection, amount), and structure (arrangement, relationship). When your explanation of the message fits the details (what is said, the material used, arrangement) and the details fit the message, you have the mind of the Author/author.

Summary: The correct interpretation of the Bible is the Author/author's intended meaning as determined by an examination of the historical, literary, linguistic, and subject context that results in the overall message (truth, idea, thesis) that explains all the details and the details explain the overall message.

In the last chapter, we discovered that there are spiritual requirements for understanding the Bible. In this chapter, it has become evident that because of the way God has chosen to record His truth (historical situations, types of literature, and language), there are some intellectual requirements, in the sense that interpreters have to think!

The Bible is unique in that it is both a divine and a human book. It has, in the words of Kuist, "two sides" (Kuist, p. 25). The Bible is a spiritual book authored by the Holy Spirit and, therefore, spiritual requirements apply to anyone who would experience and explain its message. The other side is that the Bible is a book, and like any other book, sacred or secular, certain "regulations" apply to interpret it. Both of these dimensions must be kept in perspective as we approach the Scripture. Both have a direct bearing on the understanding of the Bible.

Traina says that because the Bible deals with spiritual matters, interpretation requires spiritual sensitivity and because it is a library of books, each of which is written by a different person in a different historical situation using different terminology and different literary forms, interpretation must also utilize these and related considerations (Traina, pp. 163-164).

Without spiritual sensitivity, our approach may become mechanically academic and even critical. Without a "scientific" approach to the Scripture, our understanding of it may be merely mystical and intuitive. There should be no divorce between spiritual sensitivity and scientific sanity. Meeting the spiritual requirements and following specific regulations are essential to arriving at a correct understanding of the Bible. As Traina claims, the interpreter of the Bible needs spiritual sense and common sense (Traina, pp. 136-137).

We have explored the spiritual prerequisites in detail (see the last chapter). Since the Bible is also a "human" book, what are the other requirements for correct interpretation? Traina makes the observation that "The ability to analyze life in general often coincides with the ability to gain profound insights into the Scripture and vice versa (Traina, p. 139).

In his book, *Biblical Hermeneutics*, Terry lists intellectual and educational, as well as, spiritual qualifications (Terry, pp. 151-158). He says, "A large proportion of the sacred volume is sufficiently simple for the child to understand, and the common people and the unlearned may find on every page much that is profitable for instruction in righteousness, there is also much that requires, for its proper apprehension and exposition, the noblest powers of intellect and the most ample learning" (Terry, p. 151).

Under the topic of intellectual qualifications, Terry mentions having a "sound, well-balanced mind." He points out that some people are given to "hasty judgment," and others are "constitutionally destitute of common sense." He adds that such "mental defects disqualify one for the interpretation of the word of God" (Terry, p. 151).

Intellect, Terry says, is needed to not only understand the meaning of words and phrases but also "the drift of the argument." For example, one must be able to discern the "unity" and the "scope" of an epistle so that the picture of the whole can be seen. The "connection of thought" and the "association of ideas" must be discerned. The interpreter needs the "power of analysis" to comprehend the relationship of the parts to the whole. Imaginative power is needed, because the interpreter "must often transport himself into the past, and picture in his soul the scenes of ancient times." That calls for a "disciplined imagination." Therefore, "sound and sober judgment" is needed. One must have the ability to "analyze, examine, and compare." He adds, "The Bible comes to us in the forms of human language and appeals to our reasoned judgment; it invites investigation and condemns a blind credulity. It is to be interpreted as we interpret any other volume, by a rigid application of the laws of language, and the same grammatical analytic" (Terry, p. 153).

As far as educational qualifications, Terry says that the interpreter must be acquainted with the geography of Palestine, familiar with history, and know about chronology, customs, as well as the languages used in the Bible (Terry, pp. 154-156).

Spiritually, interpreters need "a disposition to seek and know the truth" and since the Scripture was written by the Holy Spirit, the interpreter must be "a partaker of the same Spirit." As Paul prayed in Ephesians 1:17-18, interpreters must never cease to pray for enlightenment (Terry, pp. 156-158).

Terry, of course, is correct. There are intellectual and educational requirements to fully understanding the Bible. As Traina says, "Since biblical interpretation is basically a rational process, the mind must function properly if it is to be valid" (Traina, p. 19).

Jesus says we are to love God with our mind (Mt. 22:37).

Let's review. The Bible contains spiritual truths about God and His ways. To understand it, we must have a spiritual nature, which comes only when we trust Jesus Christ and are born into the family of God. Also, God's children must depend on God's Spirit to understand God's Word. At the same time, the spiritual truth in the Bible was written in a historical situation using various literary forms and several different languages. Therefore, history, literature, and language must be taken into consideration.

Where is the Holy Spirit in interpretation? For one thing, He is the Author of all Scripture (1 Pet. 1:21; 1 Cor. 2:12-13; 2 Tim. 3:16). That means that all Scripture ultimately has the same Author and, therefore, the job of the interpreter is to determine what God meant by what is written. It also means that the Holy Spirit used historical situations, literary forms, and languages to record God's truth.

In addition, the Holy Spirit not only produced the Scripture through men, He illuminates people so that they can understand what is written (Ps. 119:18; Eph. 1:18). That does not mean that the Holy Spirit communicates apart from the words of Scripture. When the Holy Spirit illuminates, He causes the reader to see what is plainly said on the pages of the Word of God. It was there all along, but prior to the illumination of the Spirit of God, the reader did not see it. Correct interpretation is determined by the Author/author's intended meaning of the words of the text.

Correct Interpretation

To understand God's eternal, spiritual truth, which is wrapped in historical, literary and linguistic contexts, the students must unwrap the package. They must work through the history, literature, ideas, and language to get to the treasure inside.

The process of interpretation begins with an idea of what the author means. That initial interpretation is tentative and must be verified by 1) the historical situation, 2) the meaning of the type of literature, 3) the subject being discussed, 4) the meaning of the syntactical arrangement of words, and 5) the meaning of the words themselves. As each of these elements is considered, the tentative interpretation will either remain the same, be altered, or be rejected. If it is altered or discarded the new possibility must be confirmed by all the components of the passage or it too must be replaced. The correct interpretation, the one the author intended to communicate, is the one that explains all the details and the details support that interpretation.

The approach to Bible study that follows is designed to force the interpreter to consider all of the elements for a correct interpretation and to consider these elements in the order that will most likely keep the interpreter in the context of the passage.

PART II

UNDERSTANDING SPIRITUAL TRUTH

Chapter 5

WHERE TO START

In studying most books, the place to begin is on page one. Starting on page one, students systematically work their way through the book, page by page, until they come to the end. There are exceptions. Students using reference books, such as dictionaries and encyclopedias, begin somewhere in the middle. Where does a serious student of the Bible begin a study of the Bible?

Not with Word Studies

Serious Bible students often "cut their teeth" on word studies. They take one word and study all the passages where that word occurs. Word studies can be productive and profitable, but if not done correctly, word studies can be misleading.

For example, the word "ball" can mean many different things. It can be used literally or figuratively. It can be used literally of a ball in a game. It can be used figuratively of a dance. If used literally, it can refer to a small round object (a golf ball), a medium-sized round object (baseball), a large round object (basketball), or an object that is not even round at all but oblong (football). It can refer to a dance or a good time if used figuratively.

The meaning of a word is not determined by its etymology (its root meaning) or even its history (how it was used through the centuries). Studying all the occurrences of a word does not determine how it is used in a particular place. No matter how a word is used in other situations, its meaning in any given passage is determined by its use in that particular situation. One of the most fundamental laws of language is that the definition of a word is determined by its context.

Not with Sentences

A word's meaning is determined by its context, often more extensive than the sentence. For example, what does the sentence "The door is open" mean? The door could be a huge door on a large cathedral or a small door on a dollhouse. The author of the statement could mean that the door was standing wide open, standing ajar, or merely unlocked. Furthermore, such a sentence could be a statement giving information about the position of the door, a command to shut the door, or an invitation to come through the door. Based on the illustration of the door, Johnson says, "The more that is said, the less ambiguous the words are likely to be. Because of this, a whole literary unit such as a book, which would contain many clues, is seldom capable of two unrelated senses" (Johnson, p. 39).

Study Individual Books

The nature of the Bible should determine the basic unit of study. The nature of the Bible is that it consists of sixty-six books. The word "Bible" comes from the Latin word for "books" (Johnson, p. 93). The Bible is not a book; it is a library of books.

God wrote this library of books, one book at a time. Should we not study it as He wrote it? Is it not critical for us to interpret each statement of Scripture in light of the book in which it appears so that we do not misinterpret what is said? One of the most important factors in staying in context is staying in the context of the individual book. Each book is the basic context of a statement in the Bible.

Traina argues that since the Bible is a library of books, "the basic unit of study is the book" (Traina, p. 23). He even argues that each word's context in a book is the book itself (Traina, p. 145). Johnson concurs, "A book is the only independent unit of the text with a single meaning determined exclusively by the author." He adds, "So it is theologically wise to begin with the book as a whole" (Johnson, pp. 34-35 fn.). He also says that since the book alone "corresponds to the message determined by the author," the interpreter should logically begin with it (Johnson, p. 93).

Start with the Big Picture

Assuming the basic unit of study is a book, where should the study of a book begin? The study of the Scripture should move from the whole to the parts. Johnson says, "The understanding of a particular is always conditioned by an understanding of the whole" (Johnson, p. 63). In other words, instead of starting at the bottom and trying to work up (doing word studies and moving up to the meaning of a book), start at the top and work down, that is, study the book as a whole to correctly interpret the details. Johnson argues, "The process legitimately goes, not from the smallest unit to the larger ones, but from the largest context to the smaller ones" (Johnson, p. 10). Get the "big picture" first.

"Martin Luther's approach to Bible study was the same as how

how he gathered apples. First, he would shake the whole tree to let the ripe fruit fall. Then, he would climb the tree and shake each limb. Next, he would move to the branches on each limb of the tree. Then, he would shake each twig. Finally, he looked under each leaf" (Jensen, p. 107).

If people understood the historical background, the literary type, and the message of a book, they would understand each part of the book in its context. Gray put it like this: "Like the expert mountain climber, let us take people to the highest peak first, that they may see the whole range, and then they can intelligently and enthusiastically study the features of the lower levels in their relation to the whole. The opposite plan is confusing and a weariness to the flesh. Get people to see for themselves what the Bible is in the large, and then they will have a desire to see it in detail. Put a telescope in their hands first, and a microscope afterward" (Gray, p. 29).

More specifically, the following procedure enables the student of Scripture to work through the form to the substance in a systematic, methodical fashion:

- A historical survey will reveal the historical background of a particular book.
- A book synopsis will indicate the subjects covered in each book.
- Unit analysis will disclose the type of literature and the message of each literary unit in a book.
- Textual exposition explains God's ideas, as do word studies.
- Book synthesis puts the biblical book into a meaningful whole.

Such an approach would look like this:

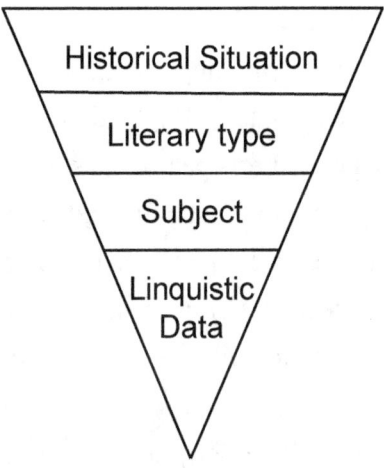

Modern books are designed to give readers an overview. They contain a summary on the jacket of the book, a table of contents, and title pages. Unfortunately, the authors of biblical books did not do that. Nevertheless, there is a way to get an overview of a book of the Bible. Start with a historical survey. Then, do a book synopsis, a unit analysis, a sentence examination, and, if necessary, a word study.

Summary: The place to begin a serious study of the Bible is with an overview of an individual book.

Let me illustrate. What is the meaning of the word "ball?" It depends on the historical, literary, subject, and linguistic context. If it is found in The London Times, on the sports page, in an article about soccer with the prefix "foot" attached, it is a round football called a soccer ball. If it is seen in The New York Times, on the sports page, in an article about the New York Giants, it is an oblong ball called a football. In the society section of the paper, the word "ball" could refer to a dance!

The issue in understanding written material is context, including the historical context (England or America), the literary context (society page or sports page), the subject context (a dance or a ball game), and the linguistic context (round ball or oblong ball). Moreover, it seems logical that the place to begin is the broader context since it determines the meaning of the details. In England, the word "football" means a round ball on the sports page.

Thus, in the study of the Scripture, it is best to begin with the broad context of the historical situation, the type of literature, the message being discussed, and the words. That way, the words of the Bible will be kept in their historical, literary, thematic, and linguistic context. The context must reign over the text!

Chapter 6

HISTORICAL SURVEY

God has chosen to reveal His truth in a historical setting. Therefore, understanding the historical situation in which a spiritual truth is revealed often gives insight into what that truth means. Historical data is more important in some books than others, but with a few exceptions, understanding the historical situation will enable anyone to understand the message of an individual book better.

Warren and Shell put it like this: "It is much easier to understand and appreciate a play if all the props and background scenes are in place. The actors on the stage perform against the background of the props and painted scenes. It is the same way with Scripture. God's revelation was given in the midst of history and the 'dramatis personae' of the Bible act out their God-given roles against the background of their times. We understand the Word of God more clearly when we see it against the backdrop of the days in which it was written" (Warren and Shell, p. 140).

A historical survey is used to determine the historical data of a biblical book. A historical survey reconstructs the historical circumstances and situation as much as possible to better understand the purpose and context of the message of a book of the Bible. It is not just "returning to the scene of the crime;" it is, as much as possible, "reenacting the crime." It pinpoints the circumstances that provoked the author to write.

Different types of historical background information are beneficial. The general historical period places a particular biblical book in one of ten periods of biblical history. The particular historical situation focuses on issues such as the author, the original audience, and the purpose for writing. Specific historical events and practices outside the Bible shed light on statements in the Scripture.

To amass the pertinent historical data of a book of the Bible, follow these steps:

Determine the Historical Period

The Historical Periods The Bible can be divided into ten historical periods. (See The Plane View of the Bible in the "The Basic Bible course" at the disciplesinstitute.com).

1. The Period of the Patriarchs
2. The Period of the Exodus
3. The Period of the Conquests
4. The Period of the Judges
5. The Period of the United Kingdom
6. The Period of the Divided Kingdom
7. The Period of the Captivity
8. The Period of Restoration
9. The Period of the Ministry of Christ
10. The Period of the Acts of the Apostles

Historical Survey

As a student of the Scripture, you should have this historical outline of the Bible firmly fixed in your mind. You should be able to rattle it off as you can the alphabet or your Social Security number. It will enable you to think through the Bible historically. In addition, it will facilitate putting each book of the Bible in its historical setting.

In Which Period Did the Events Happen? At the beginning of the study of any biblical book, the student should ask, "During what historical period did the events of this particular book take place?" For example, most of the book of Genesis took place during the Period of the Patriarchs. The events of Exodus and Numbers happened during the Period of the Exodus. These are rather obvious, as are books like Samuel, Kings, Ezra, and Nehemiah. Sometimes, it is not as obvious as in the case of some of the prophets of the Old Testament. With only a few exceptions, the books themselves identify the period in which they took place.

In Which Period was the Book Written? With the majority of the books of the Bible, the historical period of the events of the book and the historical period of the writing of the book are the same, but there are exceptions. It is important to note an exception.

For example, the events recorded in Genesis took place during the Period of the Patriarchs, but it was not written until the Period of the Exodus. The events of Judges happened during the Period of the Judges, but Judges was probably not written until almost the beginning of the United Kingdom. All four Gospels record events that took place during the Period of the Ministry of Christ, but none of the Gospels were written until or after the Period of the Acts of the Apostles.

In these cases, there is a time-gap between the event and the recording of the event. Therefore, the student should ask, "Why was there such a gap? What circumstances brought about the writing of events that happened previously to the time in which the author wrote (and lived)?"

Let me illustrate. Most of the events in the book of Genesis occurred during the Period of the Patriarchs, but the book was not written until more than 400 years later, during the Period of the Exodus. What was going on in the Period of the Exodus that provoked Moses to write about the Period of the Patriarchs? Was he writing in general to tell the curious how the world began and how humans were created? Obviously not. That is only a very small portion of the fifty chapters of the book of Genesis.

When Genesis was written, Moses was leading the children of Israel out of Egypt to the Promised Land. They needed to know that the Creator God of the universe had promised their ancestors, the patriarchs, namely Abraham, Isaac, and Jacob, the land of Canaan. Thus, Genesis was written during the Period of the Exodus to explain to the children of Israel where they were going and why. It also explains how they ended up in Egypt.

How Does the Period Relate to the Book? After determining the historical period during which the book took place and the period during which the book was written, the question needs to be asked, "How does the historical period(s) relate to the book?" For example, the historical period of any of the prophets needs to be determined to thoroughly understand what is going on in each book. Did this prophet live and minister during the Period of the Divided Kingdom, the Captivity, or the Restoration? How did the circumstances of these periods relate to this particular major or minor prophet?

First and Second Chronicles are books that were not written during the period in which the events happened. They were written during the Restoration period, but they cover several historical periods before that time. The author is reaching back into history to demonstrate God's concern for the Temple to teach his generation the importance of rebuilding the Temple.

How does one determine the general historical period of a biblical book? Appendix 2 gives the dates for each period and the biblical books covered in each period. Any good study Bible will give this information in the introduction of the book. A Bible dictionary will do the same, as will the introductory sections of most commentaries.

Describe the Historical Situation

Determining the historical period only indicates the general situation of the period when the events of the book took place. The particular historical situation of each book needs to be ascertained.

Authors do not write in a vacuum. They write about a specific subject with a particular audience in mind. Authors write about subjects "occasioned by a historical audience" (Johnson, p. 85). That is true of the books of the Bible. "The letters of the New Testament, like the prophecies of the Old, were addressed to specific assemblies struggling with particular problems" (Robinson, p. 27).

Certain basic questions need to be asked and answered to identify the immediate historical situation. Rudyard Kipling's classic statement serves as a guide.

> I have six faithful serving men
> Who have taught me all I know
> Their names are what, where, and when
> And how and why and who

Who Ask, "Who wrote this particular book?" Sometimes, the human author of a biblical book is not important. In fact, there are times when God does not even bother to tell us who the human author was! Apparently, we do not need to know. For instance, we do not know for certain who wrote Judges, Ruth, 1 Samuel, 2 Samuel, 1 Kings, 2 Kings, 1 Chronicles, 2 Chronicles, Esther, Job, many of the Psalms, and the book of Hebrews.

In other instances, however, knowing the human author can be valuable. A simple illustration is Psalm 51. Knowing that David, who had committed adultery with Bathsheba, is the author of this extensive confession is useful information in understanding the Psalm.

The author of the third Gospel was Luke. As a doctor, it is significant that he included the story of the virgin birth. When he records Jesus' statement of the camel going through the eye of the needle, he uses the Greek word for a surgeon's needle, indicating that Jesus was referring to an actual needle and not a hole in the wall of Jerusalem.

If James, the half-brother of Jesus Christ, is the author of the book of James, his identification of himself in the first verse becomes very impressive. Instead of calling himself an apostle or the half-brother of Jesus, he identifies himself as a slave of God and of the Lord Jesus Christ.

The other "who" question that needs to be asked is, "To whom was the book written?" The more that is understood about the recipients of a book, the better the understanding of that book. In many cases, it is not going too far to say that understanding the recipients of the book is the key to understanding the book. The original recipients often had a problem that provoked the writing of a book. The author had a message, a timeless truth from God, which dealt with their situation and similar situations. Therefore, understanding the original historical situation will give insight into the author's message and meaning. The student needs to ask such questions as: what were the recipients' characteristics and conditions, for what were they commended, and what seemed to be their problem(s)?

Obviously, the book of Galatians was written to the Galatians, but what were they like? What were their circumstances? What were their problems? From the book itself, we know they were believers. Paul asks, "Did you receive the Spirit by the works of the law, or by the hearing of faith?" (Gal. 3:2). Yet they were beginning to keep Jewish holy days. Paul says to them, "You observed days and months and seasons and years. I am afraid for you, lest I have labored for you in vain" (Gal. 4:10-11). They had gone so far as to contemplate being circumcised. Later in the book, Paul says, "If you become circumcised, Christ will profit you nothing" (Gal. 5:2). In fact, that seems to be the issue in the book, for when Paul comes to the close of the book, he makes the statement, "As many as desired to make a good showing in the flesh, these try to compel you to be circumcised, only that they may not suffer persecution for the cross of Christ" (Gal. 6:12). Furthermore, some questioned Paul's apostleship and authority. They charged him with being a man-pleaser (Gal. 1:10) and, therefore, he preached circumcision among the Jews but not the Gentiles (Gal. 5:11).

Isolating the historical background material in Galatians helps to understand what is happening in the book. Paul begins by defending his apostleship (chapters 1-2). He proves that justification is by faith apart from the law (chapters 3-4) and concludes by teaching that neither is sanctification by the law; it is by walking in the Spirit (chapters 5-6). His purpose is to prevent these believers from trying to keep the law, particularly circumcision, to please God. The problem in Galatia was circumcision; the book was designed to solve that problem.

When Hirsch argues that it is important to date even an anonymous text because the interpreters need all the clues they can muster concerning the cultural and personal attitudes the author might be expected to bring to bear communicating his verbal meaning (Hirsch, 1967, p. 240). Knowing the answer to the question "when" is particularly helpful when studying the Minor Prophets. Jonah was a Jew from the Northern Kingdom who lived about 760 BC. No wonder he did not want to go to Nineveh! It was the capital of Assyria, the most powerful nation on the earth at the time and a threat to the Northern Kingdom. A few years after Jonah's experience, Assyria conquered the Northern Kingdom. Jonah had every right to fear.

As mentioned before, the events of a book could have taken place in one historical period and have been written in another. So

Historical Survey

the question of "when" needs to, if necessary, cover both possibilities. As much as possible, an exact date should be determined.

The events of Genesis took place from the creation of humanity to the death of Joseph (1860 BC), but the book was not written until after the Exodus, which was in 1447 BC. Moses was not a contemporary of the events of the book of Genesis. Therefore, he probably used sources, either oral or written. The phrase "this is the book of the generation of" occurs eleven times in Genesis. Many, including conservative scholars, have suggested that these "books" within Genesis were written sources Moses used under the supervision of the Holy Spirit to pen Genesis. Did Noah write "The Genealogy of Noah" (Gen. 6:9-9:29)?

It should be noted that it is not always possible to establish the exact date for some biblical books. When it is impossible to determine the precise date, or even a close date, the Author/author does not consider the date critical to understanding what is written. In such cases, there is sufficient information of the situation to understand the message the Author/author intends to communicate. The date and even the situation of some psalms are unknown, but each psalm contains enough information to understand its message.

Where There are two parts to the "where" question. The first is, "Where was the author when he wrote the book?" and the second is, "Where were the recipients when they received the book?"

Paul wrote the book of Romans while staying in Corinth, the sin city of the ancient world. Romans 1 is no doubt a description of what Paul saw taking place in the loose and licentious city of Corinth. So, when studying Romans 1, investigate the conditions in Corinth! When Paul wrote Philippians, he was in prison.

Imagine being in prison when writing a letter that repeatedly speaks of joy and rejoicing!

The place written to or about could also be important. Obadiah wrote to Israel about Edom. Understanding the city of Petra will greatly enhance the understanding of what Obadiah had to say to the Jewish people. "You who dwell in the clefts of the rock, whose habitation is high" (Obad. 3) is a direct reference to the inhabitants of Petra. Understanding Petra makes this verse come alive.

In ancient times, the city was thought to be impregnable. From a military point of view, in Obadiah's day, Petra did seem secure. The entrance of the city was a narrow ravine a mile in length. The ravine was so narrow in places only one horse could get through at a time. The walls of rock on either side of the ravine were 700 feet high. The city was clearly able to repel an invasion. It was virtually impregnable. A direct attack, even by a superior force, was easily stopped. In such a fortress, Edom considered herself secure even from God. No wonder Obadiah said, "You who say in your heart who will bring me down to the ground" (Obad. 3). Yet, he predicted, "Though you exalt yourself as high as the eagle, and though you set your nest among the stars, from there I will bring you down, says the Lord" (Obad. 4). History reveals this is exactly what happened.

Illustrations from throughout the Scripture could be multiplied. Knowing about the city of Corinth helps us understand why things happened the way they did in the church. It is also helpful to highlight and understand things Paul told the Corinthians in that pagan, polluted city.

What What is the subject of the book? The answer to the "who" question concerning the recipients is helpful here, especially if the author is addressing their situation, but the content of the book determines the subject of the book.

At this stage of the study, it might be difficult to determine the overall subject of the entire book without a more detailed examination of the book or help from someone else. At this point, at least be aware that one of the main questions that need to be answered concerns the subject.

Why Clearly, two of the most important questions that can be asked concerning any book of the Bible are: "Who were the recipients?" and "Why was it written?" Knowing why a book was written is vitally important. Traina says, "There should be a complete mastery of the Scriptures in view of the purpose of each book and of the entire Bible" (Traina, p. 11).

Why did Moses write Genesis? Did he write to answer questions concerning origins? Hardly. It was written to the Jews during the Period of the Exodus to explain to them why they were leaving Egypt and why they were going to Canaan. The purpose of Genesis is to explain the Abrahamic Covenant and not just the creation of the world or humanity. That is why Moses gives only two chapters to creation and twelve to Abraham.

Why did the authors of the synoptic Gospels write their books? Was the purpose evangelism? Did Matthew, Mark, and Luke write to unbelievers to get them saved? If they did, why is there an absence in those three books of a clear emphasis on salvation by grace through faith? John wrote a Gospel and made it clear that a person can have eternal life only by believing. That message is conspicuous by its absence from the synoptic Gospels. Was the purpose of the synoptic Gospels, then, to give believers information concerning the ministry of Christ?

How does one determine the immediate, historical situation of a book of the Bible? With very few exceptions, virtually everything that is known today about the immediate historical background of any book in the Bible comes from that book itself. The way to determine the immediate historical background of any biblical book is to read and reread that book to answer the questions mentioned in this chapter.

Many have practiced repeated reading of a book with lasting profit. Dr. Benjamin Jowett of Oxford once said he had just finished reading Boswell's *Life of Johnson* for the fiftieth time. Charles Haddon Spurgeon said he had read *Pilgrims Progress* one hundred times. You do not have to read a biblical book that many times to do a historical survey, but you do have to read it several times. A historical survey could be done in about an hour in a short book like James. Nevertheless, there is no substitute for the repeated reading of Scripture. James M. Gray, G. Campbell Morgan, and W. Graham Scroggie were well known for applying and recommending this Bible study method.

After reading a biblical book for yourself to determine its historical background, it is helpful to read what others have written. A good reference Bible will have an introduction at the beginning of each book, giving the historical data connected with that book. Any Bible dictionary will also have a short section answering the questions concerning the historical situation of any biblical book. Look up the name of that particular book in the Bible dictionary. One of the best sources of this kind of material is the introductory section of a commentary. Pastors and laymen alike usually skip that part of the commentary, considering it technical and unrelated to the practical material of the book. However, that section gives the historical background that makes the material and the biblical book more understandable.

Discern any Specific Historical References

Some biblical books have references and allusions to external events and practices. In those cases, understanding the historical background sheds light on specific statements in Scripture. For example, in the Sermon on the Mount, Jesus said, "And whoever compels you to go one mile, go with him two" (Mt. 5:41). He is referring to a Roman law that said a Roman solider could compel people to carry their burden one mile. When the Scribes and the Pharisees were compelled to help a Roman soldier, they did it but hated it. They carried the load and counted the steps. At exactly one mile, they put the load down, refusing to go another foot, and they felt righteous because they had done what the law demanded. Jesus is teaching that they would go two miles if they had true righteousness. Rather than going one mile in anger, go two miles.

Summary: Understanding the general historical period, the particular historical situation, and any specific historical events and practices will better enable anyone to understand the message of an individual book of the Bible.

While it is not possible to answer all the historical questions for every book of the Bible, the more the historical circumstances and situations are understood, the more the purpose and content of the book will be understood. More specifically, a historical survey uncovers the factors that motivated the author to write, which, in turn, helps the modern reader understand what is written.

Traina emphatically wrote, "Because the books of the Bible were written in a specific historical setting, and because they were addressed to those who lived in a concrete, historical situation, it is imperative that one utilize their historical background if one is to recreate the message of their authors." Later, he wrote, "The beginning point of exegesis should be the meaning of a scriptural unit in its specific historical situation" (Traina, pp. 152 and 182).

Kaiser concurs, saying, "It is exceedingly important that the interpreter complete a thorough investigation of the biblical book's author, date, cultural and historical background. It is virtually impossible to locate the book's message in space and time without this essential material" (Kaiser, p. 150).

Suppose you were watching a film whose setting is the Civil War in America in the 1860s. The more you understood the history of that period, the easier it would be for you to understand and fully appreciate the film itself. It is the same with the Scriptures. God's Word was written in the midst of history. The people in the Bible thought, spoke, and acted against the background of their times. We understand the Scriptures more clearly when we see them against the backdrop of the times in which they were written.

After you have read and reread a biblical book to glean from it the historical situation and after you have read other sources, write a short summary of the historical survey of that book. In one page or less, give the period during which the events of the book took place, the name of the author, and the date the book was written. Most of the summary should focus on the recipients. From the book itself, determine what was going on in their situation. Ask such questions as what were the characteristics and conditions of the recipients, what they were commended for, and what seemed to be their problem(s).

Sir Francis Bacon (1561-1626), the English philosopher, said, "Reading maketh a full man, conference a ready man, and writing an exact man."

The following are examples of historical surveys for the books of Nehemiah and James. Notice that the material comes from the books and focuses on what is happening to the recipients.

A Historical Survey of Nehemiah

The author of the book of Nehemiah was Nehemiah (1:1). It is possible and even likely that Nehemiah compiled portions of the book (see Nch. 7:5-73). Nehemiah 2:1 indicates that Nehemiah served under Artaxerxes, who reigned in Persia from 464 through 423 BC. Nehemiah departed from Persia in the twentieth year of Artaxerxes (Neh. 2:1, 444 BC). He returned to Persia 12 years later in the 32nd year of Artaxerxes (Neh. 13:6, 432 BC). Later, he returned to Jerusalem, probably around 425 BC. Conservative scholars date the book of Nehemiah about 425 BC. It was written and took place during the Period of the Restoration.

The recipients of the book, the remnant in Jerusalem after the captivity, experienced the events of the book. Nehemiah was not written to correct some of the needs of the recipients but to remind them of what God had done among them in rebuilding the wall around Jerusalem and restoring the people to Jerusalem.

A Historical Survey of James

According to the opening verse of the epistle of James, the author was James. The problem is which James. Early tradition says it was James, the half-brother of Jesus. The information we have concerning James from the rest of the New Testament fits the picture we have from the book. For example, he speaks with authority, and the style of speech in Acts 15 fits the style of the epistle of James. The book of James was written during the Period of Acts of the Apostles.

The recipients were Jewish (Jas. 1:1) Christians (see "brethren" throughout, except Jas. 5:1-6). The book is addressed to "the twelve tribes, which were scattered abroad." This is probably a reference to the Jewish Christians who were scattered abroad because of the persecution in Acts 8:4 (Acts 9:2; 11:19). If so, they were only as far away from Jerusalem as Syria (Acts 11:19). If this identification is correct, and many conservative scholars believe it is, the date of James is about AD 45, making it the first, or one of the first books in the New Testament to be written.

From the book itself, it is obvious that these Jewish Christians were still meeting in synagogues (Jas. 2:2) and had elders (Jas. 5:14). Strangers sometimes attended their meetings (Jas. 2:2-4). While some among them were rich (Jas. 1:10), some were even traveling traders (Jas. 4:13 ff), the majority were probably poor

(Jas. 1:9; 2:6; 5:1-6).

They were having various kinds of trials. The rich were oppressing them by hauling them before the courts (Jas. 2:6-7) and wrongfully withholding their wages (Jas. 5:4). Perhaps religious persecution was involved (Jas. 2:7). Furthermore, these believers were having trouble among themselves. They had disagreements, ambitions, and strife (Jas. 3:13-18; 4:1, 2, 11). Some were weak from sickness (Jas. 5:13), probably due to God's chastening.

To make matters worse, they were not enduring their trials with joy and submission. They were being partial (Jas. 2:1-13). Many were trying to give advice, assuming the role of a teacher (Jas. 3:1). They had bitter jealousy and strife in their hearts (Jas. 3:14), causing them to misuse the tongue to abuse one another (Jas. 3:9-10), arguing with one another (Jas. 4:1), speaking against one another (Jas. 4:11), and groaning against one another (Jas. 5:9). They were lusting after things (Jas. 4:2) and were not praying properly (Jas. 4:4). Acting as if they were self-sufficient, they did not consider the will of God (Jas. 4:13, 16). Since they needed to take oaths (Jas. 5:12), it appears that they were not completely honest with each other either.

Chapter 7

BOOK SYNOPSIS

When contractors build a house, they do not build one complete room at a time. Imagine carpenters, plumbers, and electricians building a finished bathroom first, including all the plumbing and fixtures. Then, they add one completed room after another until they finish the house. That is the way some people study the Bible. They take a verse in a book or a small portion within a book and study it in detail, adding the verses around it until they have completed the whole.

The way contractors build houses is how Bible students should study the Bible. Contractors begin with the whole. Stakes are put into the ground to determine the outer limits of the house. The foundation is poured, and all of the rooms are framed before any particular room is built. In a similar fashion, students of the Scripture need to begin with the whole. The basic whole unit in the Bible is individual books. Only after students of the Scripture grasp the whole book as a unit should they delve into its details in depth. In his book *How to Study the Bible for the Greatest Profit*, R. A. Torrey said, "This method of study is the most thorough, the most difficult, and the one that yields the largest and most permanent results" (Torrey, p. 14).

After a historical survey of a biblical book, the next step is synopsis. The English word "synopsis" means "a general view." In the book synopsis, students take a picture of a book with a wide angle before they take a picture with a microlens. Book synopsis is the penthouse view, not the manhole view. The definition of a book synopsis is a brief review or summary of the whole book. It is thinking through the natural literary units of a book. It formulates a tentative concept of the message of the book.

It is important to note that a book of the Bible must be analyzed by its natural literary units, not chapters and verses. Pointing out that originally, there were no verses or chapter divisions, Mickelsen says many times, "chapter divisions artificially obscure the continuance of thought" (Mickelsen, p. 104). Ray Stedman is more emphatic. In a sermon on Romans 7:25-8:4, he says, "I believe that God inspires the text of Scriptures, 'breathed out' by Him—but I believe that the chapter divisions were put in by the devil. Many times, they come right at a place where they actually obscure the truth."

What are the natural literary units of a book? The answer to that question depends on the type of book. The natural literary unit in Old and New Testament historical books is the individual narrative or story. In historical books, particularly in the Old Testament, chapter divisions often divide the book into individual narratives. Unfortunately, there are times when that is not true, especially in the Gospels (see the one vision in Dan. 10-12; also Jn. 2:23-3:21). In the epistles of the New Testament, the literary unit is the paragraph, for example, Colossians. The literary unit may also be 1) a discourse, 2) a narrative plus a discourse, 3) a narrative plus a parable, 4) a psalm, or 5) a single proverb, etc.

If you were to walk to the top of the Washington Monument to get a bird's eye view of the Lincoln Memorial, the White House, and other sights in the surrounding area, you would have to climb 898 steps. Fortunately, one does not have to climb that many steps to get a bird's eye view of a book of the Bible. The following three simple steps will lead to the overview provided by a book synopsis study of the Scriptures.

Step One: Read the Book

Read the Book First, a word about reading the Bible. Reading has fallen on hard times in our age of poor readers, automation, TV, and computers. The problem is compounded by the fact that most Americans live in the fast lane and reading takes time.

There are no substitutes for reading the Bible. When it comes to Bible study, there is no substitute for the repeated reading of the same material. It may not take as much time as you think. Many New Testament books can be read in 15 minutes or less. If some of the epistles of the New Testament were printed in the newspaper, they would fill no more than two columns of newsprint. In fact, the longest books in the New Testament are Luke and Acts. Either one can be read by an average reader in about two hours. That may seem like a long time, but how many evenings have you spent watching TV for two hours or more?

I submit that our problem with Bible study may just be at this point. We do not even read it! A mother was trying to get her eight-year-old daughter, Mary, to learn her Sunday School lesson. At length, she took the Bible from the dresser drawer and said, "Come, Mary, I will help you learn your lesson. Then, you can go back to play." Mary replied, "All right, Mother, but let's study it from Grandfather's Bible. It's much more interesting than yours." "But, Mary," the mother objected, "they're exactly alike." "Oh," Mary replied, "I thought grandfather's might be more interesting than yours. He certainly reads it more than you do." Unfortunately, that is a commentary on all too many believers today.

The biblical approach to Bible study begins with the right person doing the studying (Part I). The next step is learning to read and reread the Scriptures. As soon as the children of Israel entered the Promised Land, they immediately "wrote on the stones a copy of the law of Moses" (Josh. 8:32). Then, Joshua "read all the words of the law ... there was not a word of all that Moses had commanded which Joshua did not read before the congregation of Israel. With the women, the little ones, and the strangers who were living among them" (Josh. 8:34-35). After that initial reading, the Word written in stone remained for all of Israel to read. Keep in mind that Moses wrote the first five books of the Bible. As soon as those books were completed and the Israelites were in the land, provision was made for all to read the Scriptures.

The last Book of the Bible ends with this promise, "Blessed is he who reads and those who hear the words of this prophecy and keep those things which are written in it for the time is near" (Rev. 1:3). In this verse, reading is public reading, but the point is God wants people to hear His Word. From the beginning to the end of the Bible, God makes clear that He wants His people to read (and/or hear) what He wrote.

He wrote His Word by books. Did He not, therefore, intend that we read it a book at a time? From a practical point of view, it is

Book Synopsis

indispensable that a particular book is read and reread to ascertain a historical survey and a book synopsis.

At this stage of your study, you should read a book of the Bible all the way through at one sitting and do that several times. G. Campbell Morgan said, "I have always advocated that beginners should commence with the New Testament and get a bird's eye view of each book, the simplest method being taking a book, say the Gospel of Matthew, and reading straight through at a sitting, and doing this repeatedly until the general movement of the book is grasped" (cited by Don M. Wagner in *The Expository Method* of G. Campbell Morgan).

As you read, you should look for the following.

The Subjects Covered While authors have one main, overall subject, it is also true that several different subjects support the major subject of a book. So, read a biblical book thinking about the subjects that are covered. While you may want to jot down a note or two at this stage, meticulous, accurate study is not the point. As you read, get the feel of the book. Notice in a "general" way what subjects are being discussed.

For example, as you begin to read the book of Nehemiah, you quickly discover that his concern is for the situation in Jerusalem. He becomes so burdened and concerned for the people in the city and the wall around it that he seeks permission to journey to Jerusalem to do something about the situation there. The king grants him permission. He travels to Jerusalem and makes a midnight ride around the wall. He soon gathers the people about him and challenges them to work. Nehemiah records in detail the work done on the wall, especially the work on the gates, but no sooner do they begin work on the wall than the opposition breaks out. The opposition is first from without, but it is also from within. Finally, through sheer determination and persistence, Nehemiah and the inhabitants of Jerusalem complete the wall in record time. In such a fashion, your synopsis should continue as you think your way through the rest of the book of Nehemiah.

Take another example. As you read James, you quickly discover that he discusses several different subjects. He begins with trials and jumps to temptation. He talks about the Word, prejudice, works, the tongue, unjust treatment, and sickness.

The Subject Changes In the second or third reading, pay more careful attention to the specific places where the subject changes. Jotting down a reference or two is helpful here. More meticulous and accurate study will be done later. At this point, however, noting the subject changes is useful, especially for what will be done in the next phase.

Consider Nehemiah again, but this time, instead of just noticing the subjects covered, notice where the subject changes. Nehemiah's concern was for the situation in Jerusalem (chapter 1). He became so burdened and concerned for the people of the city and the wall around it that he sought permission from the king to journey to Jerusalem and do something about the situation there. The king granted him that permission. He traveled to Jerusalem and made a midnight ride around the wall. He soon gathered the people about him and challenged them to work (chapter 2). Nehemiah records in detail the work done on the wall, especially the work done on the gates (chapter 3). No sooner do they start the work on the wall when opposition breaks out. The opposition is first from without (chapter 4), but it is also from within (chapter 5). Finally, through sheer determination and persistence, Nehemiah and the inhabitants of Jerusalem complete the wall in record time (chapter 6).

In the case of James, he discusses trials (1:2-12), temptation (1:13-18), the Word (1:19-27), prejudice (2:1-13), works (2:14-26), the tongue (3:1-12), wisdom (3:13-18), conflict (4:1-10), judging others (4:11-12), business trips (4:13-17), unjust treatment (5:1-12), and sickness (5:13-18).

The Main Subject Along with noting the subjects covered and where the subject changes, begin to think about what the main subject might be. At this point, the conclusions are tentative, but it is valuable to have this in mind even as you begin reading a book.

In the case of Nehemiah, it is obvious that the first several chapters revolve around the rebuilding of the wall. You might conclude that Nehemiah's subject is just the rebuilding of the wall. Be careful. That's premature. The wall was completed in chapter 6, but there are seven more chapters in the book of Nehemiah. The overall subject of Nehemiah must consider the last seven chapters. So obviously, although the building of the wall is a major part of Nehemiah, there is more to Nehemiah than that. There is also the city's repopulation and even the people's repeated restoration. Thus, the subject of the book of Nehemiah is not the rebuilding of the wall or the repopulation of Jerusalem but continual spiritual restoration. In the context of the Old Testament, this is even more apparent. Zerubbabel came and restored. Ezra came and restored. Nehemiah came and restored twice.

Determining the subject of James can be difficult. He seems to jump from one subject to another. Various topics for an overall subject have been suggested, including faith, works, and maturity. Is it significant that James begins and ends with the subject of trials (Jams. 1:2 and 5:13)? That seems to fit the result of the historical survey, namely, that the original recipients were experiencing trials.

Step Two: Title the Units

To obtain a more specific overview, the units of the book need to be accurately identified and summarized. A simple and effective way to do this is to title each unit.

Identification Determine the number of literary units. In historical material, the unit is each narrative or story. In didactic material, the unit is the paragraph. Determining the narrative units is done by reading the book and specifying the beginning and end of each story. The paragraph units can be determined by either looking at a Bible that prints the paragraphs as paragraphs or designates them in some other fashion. For example, the New King James Version prints the number of the first verse of a paragraph in bold type. Remember: paragraphs are not in the original autographs. They were added later by editors and translators. Some translators tend to have longer paragraphs than others.

Titles After identifying each unit, record a title for it. This process will help you refine your conclusions. You will discover your first observations are not always your most accurate. Most change their conclusions several times while studying a book of the Bible.

List the units and the title for each one on a piece of paper.

The great advantage of this process is that it helps you remember. Reading and rereading a book of the Bible yields much fruit, but even the best of minds will forget at least some of the details. By recording your findings, you will remember them for use later. Here is an illustration from James.

1.	1:1	Salutation
2.	1:2-12	Trials
3.	1:13-18	Temptation
4.	1:19-20	The righteousness of God
5.	1:21-27	Doing the Word
6.	2:1-13	Partiality
7.	2:14-26	Faith without works
8.	3:1-12	The tongue
9.	3:13-18	Wisdom
10.	4:1-10	The cause of conflict
11.	4:11-12	Judging
12.	4:13-17	Planning
13.	5:1-12	Unjust treatment
14.	5:1318	Sickness
15.	5:19-20	Restoration

Step Three: Read What Others Have Written

You should do your own work first, but to check your accuracy as well as gain additional insight, see what others have done. The introductory sections of commentaries, especially the more technical ones, often give a book synopsis. Some call it just that. Others call it "analysis."

Commentaries and the introduction section of each biblical book in a study Bible give an outline. These outlines are a form of a synopsis.

Summary: After doing a historical survey, the next step in studying a book is getting a synopsis of it.

Having done a historical survey and a book synopsis, you now have a feel for the situation that provoked the author to write and a general idea of all he had to say. That will help you understand each individual literary unit throughout the book. It will also help keep you in context.

At the same time, there is a sense in which this general idea is tentative. This initial concept may be altered as the various literary units are analyzed. So, each literary unit needs to be carefully analyzed. That is the next step.

Chapter 8

UNIT ANALYSIS

God has chosen to produce His Word in the form of books. These books ought to be our major concern in understanding the Bible, but it is hard to digest an entire book, especially at the beginning of the study of that book. To digest the whole, we divide it into smaller parts. Beef is a form of food, but it is difficult to digest a whole cow. Therefore, we divide it into T-bone steaks, roast, and filet mignon. These are digestible portions. In a similar fashion, we need to divide books into their parts. We need to analyze the various units of the books of the Bible.

The dictionary defines analysis as "separating into parts to discover their nature, function, and relationship." The definition of unit analysis is that it is the study of the parts of a natural literary unit of a biblical book to determine its message. Each literary unit in a biblical book has a message, which should be summarized in a single sentence. That message, combined with all the others in the book, contributes to the overall message of the book. So, with insight into the circumstances gained from the historical survey and with the tentative concept of the book's message in mind, each literary unit should be analyzed to find its contribution to the book's overall message.

As we have seen, literary units consist mainly of narratives or paragraphs. Thus, unit analysis studies the parts of the narrative or the parts of a paragraph. The parts of a paragraph are sentences. So, unit analysis of a paragraph will pay particular attention to the relationship of the sentences within that paragraph. This approach to Bible study attempts to put all the parts in each unit into a meaningful whole. Later, in book synthesis, the relationships of the units themselves to each other will be considered.

Here are several methods that may be utilized in analyzing a literary unit of Scripture.

Observe the Type of Literature

Before interpreting any passage, the type of literature used must be determined. As we have seen, literature is the artistic arrangement of human experience in written form. Literature is concerned with not only what is said but how it is said. When Jesus sent out the twelve, He told them that when they were persecuted, they were not to worry about what to say or how to say it (Mt. 10:19). In other words, they were not to be concerned about the substance or the form or of what is to be said. In their case, the Holy Spirit would assist them in what to say and how to say it.

The Bible contains various types of literary forms, such as narrative, poetry, proverbs, prophecy, parable, and epistle. Each of these literary forms (genre) has its own distinct structure. Understanding these literary forms is critical to understanding what is written. Therefore, it is imperative to understand the various types of literature used in Scripture.

That is true of all written material. Hirsch says, "Before we interpret a text, we often classify it as casual conversation, lyric poem, military command, scientific prose, occasional verse, novel epic, and so on. In a similar way, I have to classify the object I see as a box, a sphere, a tree, and so on before I can deduce the character of its unseen or inexplicit components" (Hirsch, 1967, p. 222).

This is an aspect of the Scripture that is often overlooked. Do not skip it. Ryken explains, "When a writer sits down to write, he asks not only what do I want to say, but also, how do I wish to say it? What kind of artifact do I desire to make? By the same token, the reader must be ready to respond to the artistic elements of literature. In general, beauty of form is as essential to literature as is the truthfulness of content" (Ryken, p. 13).

Ramm says, "An appreciation of literary genre is indisputable for the understanding of Scripture because so much of Scripture (in a sense all of Scripture) is expressed in some kind of literary genre" (Ramm, p. 142). Later, Ramm says that no book of the Bible can be intelligently interpreted without first noting its literary genre (Ramm, pp. 146-147).

Frankly, the literary genre of the Bible is a field of study by itself. Whole books have been written on this subject. The following briefly describes the major types of literature in God's Word.

Narrative Literature Narrative is the most dominant type of literature in the Bible (Johnson, p. 168). A narrative is a story, a unified sequence of events. The storyteller selects material and proportionately arranges it to make a point. The historical books in the Old Testament and the Gospels in the New Testament are of this type.

The basic story pattern consists of characters, conflict, complication, climax, and conclusion, or denouement. First, characters are introduced, followed by conflict, complications ("the plot thickens"), climax, and conclusion. Of course, narrators may choose not to follow that exact order. They may, for example, begin with the conflict and then, introduce the characters, or they may begin with the conclusion and flashback to the beginning of the story. There is an old distinction that the story is the chronology of events apart from the way the author arranges them and the plot is the order of events arranged in the story by the storyteller. The story can and does, especially in the Bible, contain dialogue.

Why do authors put their message in story form? What is the significance of the story form? Stories convey messages by example rather than by explicit statement. The example may be good or bad. The characters in the story may be individuals to emulate or people who make choices to be avoided. The lesson may be stated at the beginning, somewhere within the story, at the end, or not at all.

Stories have universal appeal. The human heart of the young and the old cries, "Tell me a story." Stories are also easy to remember. Paul told the Corinthians the "story" of the Macedonians (2 Cor. 8:1-5) to teach and to motivate (2 Cor. 8:8). This sort of literature appeals primarily to the imagination and to the emotions (Traina, p. 69).

Therefore, the interpreter should ask: 1) Who are the characters? 2) Are two of the characters in contrast to each other? 3) What are their choices? 4) What are the consequences? 5) What are the conflicts? 6) How are the conflicts resolved? 7) What does this setting contribute to the story? (For additional questions, see Haddon W. Robinson, *Biblical Preaching*, p. 69.)

The narratives in the Bible are historical narratives. No history can be exhaustive. All historical narratives are selective (Ramm, p. 181). The composition of historical stories limits the author to the two techniques of selection and arrangement. Discovering these features is critical to the interpretation of narrative literature (Johnson, pp. 116-117). Also, the biographical material in the Bible is not just character sketches of people. They are an example of spiritual truth, especially examples of people's relationship or lack of relationship to the Lord.

Poetry Poetry is a much more concentrated artistic form of literature than discourse; indeed, it is the most concentrated form of writing. Whereas the basic unit of a story is an episode or scene, the basic unit of poetry is usually said to be the image. The poet packs sentences with images, symbols, allusions, metaphors, similes, and emotive vocabulary and artistically arranges them in a poem.

Poets from different cultures have also used various literary techniques. English poetry employs rhythm and rhyme. Hebrew poetry does not. The basic poetic technique of Hebrew poetry is parallelism. Parallelism, unlike rhyme, survives in translation. Robert Frost said, "Poetry is what gets lost in translation." That is true with the rhythm and rhyme of English poetry but not with the parallelism of Hebrew poetry. Is that why God used parallelism and not rhyme in His Word?

Hebrew parallelism consists of thought arrangement rather than word arrangement. Three types of parallelism can be found in the poetry of the Old Testament.

Synonymous parallelism is the repetition of the same thought in different words. The second line of the poem says the same thing as the first, using different expressions.

> Therefore, the ungodly shall not stand in the judgment
> Nor sinners in the congregation of the righteous (Ps. 1:5).

Antithetical parallelism is the repetition of a contrasting thought. The second member of the couplet states the opposite of the first. It introduces a contrast or states the truth of the first negatively.

> For the Lord knows the way of the righteous
> But the way of the ungodly shall perish (Ps. 1:6).

Synthetic parallelism is a progressive flow of thought. The second (and maybe the following) line either explains the first or adds something. The second adds a new thought to the first.

> He shall be like a tree planted by the rivers of water
> That brings forth its fruit in its season
> This leaf also shall not wither
> And whatever he does shall prosper (Ps. 1:3).

In other words, the statements or phrases interpret each other. Therefore, it is crucial to understand the type of parallelism being used.

Unit Analysis

Poetry also expresses emotion. "Poetry is the emotions of life made audible'" (Traina, p. 69). It contains thought and reflection but is primarily a vehicle of intense emotion. Hence, the use of hyperbole (the conscious exaggeration to communicate strong feelings), exclamatory idioms, emotive words, and vivid descriptions are designed to stimulate emotion. The Psalms express the deep, spiritual feelings of praise, adoration, awe, joy, sorrow, and depression.

It is important to remember that poetry expresses feelings rather than rigid logical concepts. At the same time, poetry has logic, purposeful selection, and literary structure. Traina says, "Good poetry is not illogical and without purpose. It is true that it appeals primarily to emotions, but it is still an expression of the mind. One must, therefore, attempt to keep the emotional and logical elements in balance in its interpretation" (Traina, p. 129).

Beware of rigid analysis when explaining Hebrew poetry, such as the Psalms. Do not try to make two different thoughts out of the two lines of a synonymous parallelism. Be sure to capture the emotion, which is an integral part of poetry.

The interpreter should ask: 1) What emotions does the poet express? 2) What is the meaning of the figures of speech? 3) What is the meaning behind the images?

Proverb A proverb is a concise statement of a general truth. It is literature in the smallest possible unit, one short, pithy sentence. Proverbs are memorable.

The great danger in interpreting a proverb is to make a universal, absolute law out of it. The Bible does contain laws such as "You shall not commit adultery." This law is a universal, absolute truth applicable in all situations at all times. There are no exceptions. A proverb is not a law; it is an axiom, which is usually true in most situations, but there may be an exception. For example, one proverb in the Bible states, "For the drunkard and the glutton will come to poverty" (Prov. 23:21). That axiom is not absolute. There are exceptions. Some wealthy people are drunks and gluttons, but as a general rule, that is not true because people who lack the discipline to control their appetite will usually not have the discipline to control their money.

Parable The Greek word translated "parable" comes from two words, "beside" and "throw." The verb form means "to lay beside, compare," and the noun means "placing beside, comparison, illustration, analogy, parable." Thus, a parable consists of two parts: the spiritual truth, which is being illustrated, and the physical narrative, which is placed beside it (Traina, p. 71). A parable is a short, simple story with a moral lesson. While there are a few other parables in the Scripture, most occur in the teachings of Jesus.

If a story today begins with, "Once upon a time in a far-away land there lived a fairy princess," it would not be taken literally as historical fact. Parables are like that. They are fictitious short stories. They do not make use of talking animals. They reflect the real-life experiences of people.

Parables "arouse attention" and "etch themselves on the memory" (Tan, p. 148). They appeal to the imagination and involve the hearer in the situation. They are meant to stimulate thought, to provoke reflection, and to lead people to a decision (Vincent Taylor, *The Gospel According to Mark*, p. 250). They entice the hearer to judge the situation and challenge them to apply that judgment to themselves. In a sense, they take on the character of an argument (William L. Lane, *The Gospel According to Mark*, p. 151). The parables of Jesus are designed to test the spiritual responsiveness of the hearers (R. Allan Cole, *Mark*, p. 88).

There are two extremes in the interpretation of parables. On the one hand, everything in the parable is considered significant. The error of making everything in a parable significant was exposed by Augustine, who said that the whole plow is needed in plowing, but the plowshare alone makes the furrow and the whole frame of an instrument is useful, but the strings alone produce the music (J. A. Alexander, *Commentary on the Gospel of Mark*, p. 86). Since the classic discussion of A. Julicher, in 1899, the consensus is that a parable has one and only one point (Taylor, p. 249). A parable is a story with one main point, but it would be a mistake to conclude that the details are never significant.

When interpreting parables, several things should be kept in mind. As a general rule, a parable teaches one essential truth. "A parable, like regular figures of speech, has but one central truth" (Tan, p. 148), "one chief point of comparison" (Mickelsen, p. 224). The golden rule of parabolic interpretation is to "determine the one central truth the parable is attempting to teach" (source unknown).

Beware of trying to make everything in the parable mean something. A story with significance in every detail is an allegory, not a parable. Parables are stories with one main point: the details do not necessarily have meaning. In other words, "Do not make a parable walk on all fours" (Ramm, p. 283). In this commentary on Matthew 9:17, Alexander says, "In explaining Aesop's fable of the Fox and the Grapes, no one ever thinks of putting a distinctive meaning on the grapes, as a particular kind of fruit, or on the limbs of the Fox as having each its own significance" (J. A. Alexander, *The Gospel According to Matthew*, pp. 263-264).

There are, however, parables where some of the details have meaning. For example, in the parable of the husbandman (Mt. 21:23-39), it is evident that the landowner represents God, the vineyard represents Israel, the servants represent the prophets, and the son is Jesus Christ. At the same time, it is equally apparent that not all of the details have meaning. The parable says the landowner sent His son, "saying, 'They will respect my son'" (Mt. 21:37), but God knew they would not respect His Son.

The interpretation of a parable is often given, or clues to its interpretation can be found in the context (Ramm, p. 284). For example, the Lord Himself interprets the parable of the sower (Mt. 13:18 ff.). Luke introduces the lost sheep, coin, and son parables with a word about the setting that explains them (Lk. 15:1-2). These parables were given to explain why the Lord was eating with publicans and sinners. The individuals, or objects, in a parable are used figuratively. For example, the prodigal in the parable of the prodigal son represents the sinners with whom Jesus ate (Lk. 15:1-2).

Prose Discourse or prose is technically not literature as such. It lacks the artistic arrangement of literature proper. Didactic material addresses the audience directly, states the truth in propositional form, and uses logic and argumentation. Ideas are developed. There is a logical development of thought, a train of thought. Grammar can be critical. "This type of literature appeals primarily to the intellect" (Traina, p. 69). Biblical examples include the prophetic sermons in the Old Testament, the discourses of Jesus, and the epistles of the New Testament.

While the letters of the New Testament are didactic, written material conveys information, they also contain several literary elements. The letters of the New Testament are seasoned with rhetorical questions (a rhetorical question is asked for effect, not to elicit information), figures of speech, repetition, contrast, triplets, personification, etc.

To interpret discourse: trace the author's argument or explanation step-by-step and summarize the overall message in one sentence.

Type The Greek word for "type" means "impression," that is, "the stamp made from a dye," hence, "figure, image, example, pattern." A type is a person, thing, or event used as an example, model, or pattern. To say of a teacher, "She is a salesperson," means she has a salesperson type of personality; she is an example or pattern of a salesperson.

Campbell defines a biblical type: "A type is an Old Testament institution, event, person, object, or ceremony which has reality and purpose in biblical history, but which also by divine designs foreshadows something yet to be revealed" (Campbell, p. 250). What is interpreted in the Old Testament as type is not "foreign or peculiar or hidden" to the text of the Old Testament but rises naturally out of it (Ramm, p. 223). The connection between the Old Testament item and its New Testament counterpart "must not be accidental or superficial but real and substantial" (Ramm, p. 228).

Types are illustrations (Ramm, p. 231). Types are also a "prefiguring" (Terry, p. 246). They are "prophetic symbols" (Ramm, p. 229). They are a "species of prophecy" (Davidson, quoted by Ramm, p. 229). In contrast, a symbol has "no essential reference to time" (Terry, p. 246). It is a timeless, figurative representation. A lion is a symbol of strength and does not predict anything in the future (Ramm, p. 232).

Types are similar to, but not the same as, prophecy (Campbell, p. 250). Both point to the future and are predictive in their natures. Nevertheless, there are differences. Prophecy verbally delineates the future, while types prefigure coming reality. Prophecy is couched in words and statements, and types of speech are expressed in events, persons, and acts. Prophecy is active and types are passive (Tan, p. 168).

Biblical typology can be confusing because it is backward from the way a dye and the resultant image normally work. Usually, the dye comes first; the image is the result of the dye. In the Scripture, the dye appears in the New Testament and the image appears in the Old Testament. God gave the shadow first and then the substance that produced the shadow. The Old Testament person, thing, or event is a symbol foreshadowing the reality in the New Testament.

Most types in the Old Testament are of Christ. Adam (Rom. 5:14, 17-19) and Melchizedek (Heb. 7:1-3) are types of Christ. There are, however, types of other things. The ark is a type of baptism (1 Pet. 3:21). The wilderness experience is a type of spiritual experience today (1 Cor. 10:6)

Salomon Glassius (d. 1656) proposed two types: innate and inferred. An innate type is specifically declared to be a type in the

New Testament. An inferred type is one not explicitly designed in the New Testament (Ramm, pp. 219-220). Johannes Cocceius (1603-1669) made any Old Testament event or person that resembled a New Testament parallel a type, "thereby coming close to an allegorical approach" (Osborne, vol. 4, p. 930). John Marsh (1757-1839) developed what became known as the Marsh Principle: a type is only a type if the New Testament calls it a type. Most follow either the letter or the spirit of the Marsh Principle.

The interpretation of a type differs from using typological interpretation as a method of interpretation. Tan explains, "In the interpretation of types, what is interpreted arises from the text and is shown to have a higher application of the same sense of that text. The historical reality and existence of the type is never denied. Its typical prefigurement springs from a literal, historical base. When we say that the Passover lamb of the Jews is a type of Christ (1 Cor. 5:7), we are not denying the historicity of Passover lambs vicariously slain in every Jewish home on the night of the Exodus. We have projected a higher application of the Passover lambs to Christ, the Lamb of God. Typological interpretation is, therefore, the unfolding of the literal base of the type, not the allegorization of that which is typified. Typological interpretation is the literal interpretation of types. When an Old Testament element is said to be a type of an element in the New, this does not mean that one equals the other. One element may prefigure another, and the resemblance between the two may be very close, but a type never equals its antitype. The Old Testament sacrificial lamb typifies—but does not equal—Christ" (Tan, p. 169).

Prophecy The Bible is permeated with prophecy. "It has been said that every fourth verse in the Scripture was predictive when written" (Tan, p. 25). "There is hardly a book in the Bible which is wholly devoid of the prophetic element" (Girdlestone, p. 8). The essence of prophecy is prediction, telling beforehand a future event for motivation.

Traina differentiates between a pure prediction and a prophecy. According to him, "pure prediction" is totally unrelated to the historical setting in which it was made. On the other hand, in the Old Testament, prophecy was an aspect of preaching. Its primary purpose was to support the prophet's message. Therefore, there is a relationship between the historical situation and the prophecy that came out of it (Traina, p. 177).

The form of prophecy can be a statement, a historical situation, a type, or a vision or dream containing symbols. The Bible contains hundreds of predictions given in plain statements. A simple example is: Jesus told Peter, "Assuredly, I say to you that this night before the rooster crows, you will deny Me three times" (Mt. 26:34). There are also plain predictions about Israel (see the seventy-year captivity predicted in Jer. 25:11-12, 29:10), other nations including Samaria (Micah 1:6-7), Tyre (Ezek. 26:3-16), Babylon (Isa. 13:19-21; Jer. 51:26, 43), and the Messiah (Micah 5:2). In the Old Testament, the prophets sometimes used historical situations to predict the future (Isa. 7). Dreams and visions, which include symbols, often appear in prophetic literature (Dan. 2).

God said, "I have also spoken by the prophets, and have multiplied visions; I have given symbols through the witness of

Unit Analysis

the prophets" (Hos. 12:10). A symbol represents something else, a material object that represents something non-material. Tan puts it this way, "A symbol is a representative and graphic delineation of an actual event, truth, or object. The thing that is depicted is not the real thing but conveys a representative meaning" (Tan, p. 152). He divides symbols into symbols in of words and symbols of acts (Tan, p. 152) and suggests that symbols in prophecy are the exception, not the rule (Tan, p. 155).

Therefore, the symbolic meaning is using a word to represent something else. A golf club could be a symbol on a hat for a golf tournament. "God did not choose the mode of vision to make prophecy unclear and ambiguous through figurative representations. The prophetic state is intended to help register more clearly and make more impressive the sacred revelations being given" (Tan, p. 91).

Apocalyptic literature is a specialized form of prophecy. The word "apocalyptic" comes from the Greek word for revelation. It means "uncovering." Apocalyptic literature uses symbols to predict the future. It appeals to the imagination. Daniel and Revelation are the two apocalyptic books in the Bible.

Both prophetic and apocalyptic literature are prophetic revelations. Johnson explains the difference between the two. He says, "The prophet spoke to a historic audience about an impending crisis and in terms of that crisis spoke of the final resolution. Apocalyptic writers spoke to a historic audience in the midst of crisis and suffering and gave that audience perspective by stepping above its own day and sharing a vision of the resolution of the conflict at the end of history" (Johnson, p. 165).

There are several guidelines for the interpretation of prophecy.

1. Prophecy should be interpreted literally. The Greek word "revelation" means "uncovering." Therefore, since the purpose of prophecy is to reveal, not conceal, truth, it should be assumed that prophecy should be interpreted literally, according to the normal grammatical-historical meaning of what is written. The "language of prophecy is largely nonfigurative" (Tan, p. 132). In any case, the literal meaning of a prophetic passage is the "limiting or controlling guide" (Ramm, p. 253).

2. Nevertheless, prophecy uses symbols. Those symbols have a literal meaning. Moreover, just because a prophecy contains a symbol does not mean that everything in the prophecy is symbolic (Tan, p. 156).

The author often gives the key to interpreting the symbols in the passage. Chafer says, "Where symbolism is employed in the text, it will almost, without exception, be so indicated" (Chafer, *Systematic Theology*, vol., IV, p. 259). Tan says, "The identification and interpretation of Bible figures by the Bible itself is a rule and not an exception" (Tan, p. 143) and "The best possible material for the interpretation of symbols is the immediate context in which given symbols are found" (Tan, p. 162).

Daniel and Revelation, the two great prophetic books, contain numerous symbols, but those symbols are usually explained. Terry testifies, "The symbols employed in the Book of Daniel are, happily, so fully explained that there need be no serious doubt as to the import of most of them" (Terry, p. 262). Stanton states, "When a symbol or sign does appear in the Revelation, it is often plainly designated as such in the immediate context, together with what the symbol represents" (Stanton, *Kept From The Hour*, p. 311).

Unit Analysis

For example, in Revelation 1:20, the seven stars are interpreted as representing the seven angels, and the seven lampstands stand for the seven churches. In Revelation 17:9-10, the seven-headed beast stands for the seven hills, and in Revelation 17:18, the woman is identified as the city, which rules the earth. Thus, it is evident that the images are figurative descriptions of real things.

3. Prophecy uses types. For example, a literal historical judgment may prefigure a future worldwide judgment. That is not to say there is a double sense, that is, a double meaning. To say there is a double sense is to deny the laws of language, leaving the recipient with no rules for understanding what is meant. The law of language that makes communication possible is that "No passage in any literature has more than one sense" (Kaiser, p. 64). What father would use language that goes beyond his child's ability to understand to teach his child? (Kaiser, p. 65).

Stuart insists: "We must, therefore, either concede that the usual laws of language are to be applied to the Bible, or else that it is, and can be, no proper revelation to men unless they are also to be inspired in order to understand it. For if we suppose words are to be employed and sentences constructed and interpreted in a manner entirely new and different from all that has hitherto been known or practiced, then there is no source from which we can derive rules to interpret the Bible unless it be supernatural and miraculous" (Moses Stuart, quoted by Kaiser, p. 65). Kaiser adds, "And if we choose to delay the interpreting process until the NT writers pass a decision on the matter, how shall we validate those claims of the apostles? If indeed a NT fulfillment has taken place, who is to agree when we are without any knowledge of an OT prediction—seeing such phenomena exceed the laws of language" (Kaiser, p. 65).

Therefore, there is one and only one meaning, but there may be "multiple fulfillment" (Ramm, p. 252). This is related to the area of typology (Tan, p. 179). "Milton S. Terry, who rightly rejects double sense and accepts typology, says that 'the types themselves are such because they prefigure things to come, and this fact must be kept distinct from the question of the sense of language'" (Tan, p. 181).

When the New Testament says that an event "fulfilled" an Old Testament statement, it is not always saying that the Old Testament was predicting that event. The expression "fulfilled" means "to fill to the full." Hort, of Westcott and Hort fame, says, "The idea of filling or giving fullness to is always contained in the biblical use of fulfilling." He explains that the Divine word is conceived of as receiving a completion, so to speak, in events that are to come to pass in accordance with it (see Hort's comments on James 2:23 in his commentary on James). In other words, to say that a prophecy is "fulfilled" sounds as if the prophecy was given in the past and its one and only fulfillment is now, but that is not exactly the meaning of the word. The meaning of the word "fulfill" allows for the possibility of fulfillment in the past, but now the prophecy has been filled to the full.

In other words, there was an immediate fulfillment in the Old Testament and an ultimate fulfillment in the New Testament. This does not mean that there is a double sense. As the New Testament authors looked back at the Old Testament, they saw what was written as a type that was to be fully realized in the New Testament. They saw a comparison and concluded that the New

Testament event was the ultimate example; therefore, it "filled to the full" what was said in the Old Testament (Traina, pp. 177-178).

4. The nature of prophecy involves time. After all, it is a prediction of the future. If nothing else, there is a difference between the time the prophecy is given and the time it is fulfilled. There are also instances when the prophecy itself may include two or more events that are separated in time. In some cases, two future events, which are separated by time, may be presented together, appearing as if they occur together.

To say the same thing another way, "two or more future events, which are separated in time, may be seen by the prophet in a single profile or side by side" (Tan, p. 91; see Ramm, p. 249). It is like looking at the stars. The observer groups them as they appear to the eye, not according to their actual position in space. It is like looking at a series of mountain ranges from a distance. The peaks appear to be close together or even as one when there are valleys between the mountains (Tan, p. 92).

In the synagogue at Nazareth, Jesus read Isaiah 61 and said, "Today this Scripture is fulfilled in your hearing" (Lk. 4:21). A comparison between what Isaiah wrote and what Jesus read indicates that Jesus stopped reading in the middle of a sentence (Isa. 61:2). He did not read the phrase "day of vengeance of our God." He did not read that phrase because He read what was being fulfilled "today" (Lk. 4:21) and the day of vengeance would not be fulfilled until later. In other words, there was a time gap between the prophecies in Isaiah 61, but they are grouped together as if they occur together.

Several passages place the resurrections of saints and sinners side by side: "And many of those who sleep in the dust of the earth shall awake, some to everlasting life, some to shame and everlasting contempt" (Dan. 12:2) and "Do not marvel at this; for the hour is coming in which all who are in the graves will hear His voice and come forth; those who have done good, to the resurrection of life, and those who have done evil, to the resurrection of condemnation" (Jn. 5:28-29). These passages seem to be saying that there is one general resurrection.

Revelation 20 presents an entirely different picture. It indicates that the righteous will be resurrected and shall reign with Christ for a thousand years (Rev. 20:4) and that "the rest of the dead live not again until the thousand years were finished" (Rev. 20: 5). This is called "the first resurrection" (Rev. 20:5). The two resurrections that are grouped together in Daniel 12 and John 5 are actually separated by at least a thousand years. Furthermore, the first resurrection is not a single event but a series of resurrection events. Paul's statement sustains that conclusion, "But each one in his own order: Christ the firstfruits, afterward those who are Christ's at His coming" (1 Cor. 15:23). As Tan says, "Under the single profile of the first resurrection, therefore, is to be comprehended the resurrection of Christ, the rapture-resurrection of church saints, and the resurrection of tribulation saints (such as the two witnesses of Revelation 11). It also comprehends the resurrection of Old Testament saints at the end of the tribulation" (Tan, p. 95).

5. There are two kinds of prophecy: conditional and unconditional. Conditional prophecies contain a condition humans must meet; therefore, those prophecies depend on human obedience. If the human condition is met, the prophecy will be brought to pass

Unit Analysis

and if the human condition is not met, the prophecy will not be fulfilled. The blessings and the curses of Deuteronomy are an illustration (Tan, p. 187). Ramm lists a number of conditional prophecies (Jer. 18:8, 10; 26:12-13; Jonah 3:4; Ezek. 33:13-15; 18:30-32; Ramm, p. 250). On the other hand, some prophecies depend solely on God and, therefore, are unconditional (Ps. 110:4; Mt. 26:24).

As you begin to analyze a literary unit, observe the type of literature and its characteristics. Keep that information in mind as you continue the analysis of the unit.

Types of Literature

The Name	The Essence	The Significance
Narrative	tells a story, which is a unified sequence of events	appeals to imagination gives a good or bad example
Poetry	a concentrated, artistic form of literature that uses images and expresses feelings	appeals to emotion be careful of rigid analysis
Proverb	a concise statement of a general truth, which aids memory	appeals to the will may not apply in every case
Parable	a short story with a moral lesson used for impact	appeals to intellect do not apply all the details
Prose	direct discourse	appeals to reason; traces the train of thought
Type	a model or pattern that is a form of prophecy (symbols are timeless)	uses a present person or object to convey a future reality
Prophecy	a prediction that often uses symbols, which are representations	appeals to curiosity motivates beware of current application

One other aspect of literary analysis needs to be noted. There are legitimate and illegitimate uses of literary analysis. In the name of literary criticism, some scholars have concluded that Genesis 1 through 11 is fable, not fact, or that narrative portions like 1 Kings 22 were sloppily assembled by a redactor who utilized several contradictory sources and, therefore, they are not reliable. That approach is an abuse, not the proper use of literary analysis. The biblical narrative is historical narrative, not fiction.

There are stories that are not historical. Novels are fiction; the narratives of the Bible are not novels; they are historical. Johnson observes, "Historical narrative literature is a prophetic or divinely accepted interpretation of the history of God's people from a historical point of view that instructs and challenges the reader by telling the story of what happened using the technique of narrative art" (Johnson, p. 168).

Neither are the narratives of the Bible fables, myths, or legends. The word "fable" is from the Latin word for "story." A fable is a fictitious story used to teach a moral lesson; the characters are usually animals. By definition, it is a story that is not true. The stories in the Bible are not fables (1 Tim. 1:4; 4:7; 2 Tim. 4:4; Titus 1:14; 2 Pet. 1:16).

The word "myth" comes from a Greek word that means "speech, story, legend." A myth is a traditional story with an apparent historical basis, usually explaining the origin of something or some custom, etc. The word is also used in any fictitious story. Bultmann defines myth as anything contrary to a scientific worldview (Bultmann, p. 15).

The word "legend" comes from the Latin word for "to read." A legend is a story handed down for generations and although it is not verifiable, it is popularly believed to have a historical basis. The stories in the Bible are not fables, myths, or legends. Just because a type of literature is employed does not mean that the passage is not historically accurate. Legitimate literary analysis recognizes that authors use different kinds of literature, and knowing the characteristics of various types of literature can help in interpretation.

Closely related to, but not identical with, the literary genre is the atmosphere of the passage. The atmosphere is the underlying tone or spirit of the passage (Traina, p. 71). The mood of the passage may be one of awe (Rom. 11:33-36), thanksgiving (Phil. 1:3-8), joy (2 Cor. 7:6-7), discouragement (Ps. 42:5), doubt (Mt. 11:1-3), despair (Ps. 13:1-6), fear, (Mt. 14:22-27), etc. There may be more than one mood expressed in a passage.

Barclay suggests that when Jesus told Peter, "Get behind Me, Satan!" (Mt. 16:23), "We must try to catch the tone of voice in which Jesus spoke. He certainly did not say it with a snarl of anger in his voice and a blaze of indignant passion in his eyes. He said it like a man wounded to the heart, with poignant grief and a kind of shuddering horror."

Determine the Natural Structure

Authors often use *literary devices* as the structure of what they write. Sometimes these are immediately obvious and other times, they are obscure. Knowing the literary devices while reading and rereading the literary unit can be very profitable. Of course, authors may not use literary devices as the structure. In these cases, I look for a subject change. Determine the major and minor themes of the passage. What, then, are these clues to structure?

Places The structure of Nehemiah 2 is built around places. Nehemiah was in Shushan (Neh. 2:1-8), on his way to Jerusalem (Neh. 2:9-10), and in Jerusalem (Neh. 2:11-20).

People The key that unlocks some passages of Scripture is people. Psalm 1 describes the blessed man (Ps. 1:1-3) and the ungodly man (Ps. 1:4-6). In Titus 2:1-10, Paul tells Titus to speak to the older men (Titus 2:1-2) and the older women (Titus 2:3), who in turn are to speak to the younger women (Titus 2:4-5). Titus also exhorts the young men (Titus 2:6). Paul exhorts Titus (Titus 2:7-8) and concludes by telling Titus to exhort servants (Titus 2:9-10).

Time The frame around which a passage or a large section is built may be time. For example, after the prologue of the Gospel of John, the apostle relates the events of one day right after another. He begins with the testimony of John the Baptist to the priest and Levites (Jn. 1:19-28). Then, he records the events of "the next day" (Jn. 1:29-34). After that day, he says, "Again, the next day," and writes about still another day in the life of John the Baptist (Jn. 1:35-42). Next, he says, "The following day" and records what happened on the fourth day in a row (Jn. 1:43-51). The wedding at Cana of Galilee, where Jesus turned water into wine, occurred three days after that (Jn. 2:1-11). Thus, after the prologue, John covers the first full week in the public ministry of

Unit Analysis

Jesus: the first day (Jn. 1:19-28), the second day (Jn. 1:29-34), the third day (Jn. 1:35-39), and the fourth day (1:43-51). The seventh day is recorded in John 2:1-11. In his commentary on the Gospel of John, Morris suggests a parallel between the days of creation in Genesis 1 and this opening week in the ministry of Jesus reinforced by "in the beginning," which opens both chapters. He concludes, "Jesus is to engage in a new creation."

Commands The literary structure of many passages consists of nothing more than commands. In Colossians 3:5-11, Paul exhorts his readers to 1) "Put to death your members" (Col. 3:5-7), 2) "Put off all these" (Col. 3:8), and 3) "Do not lie" (Col. 3:9-11). Paul's three commands to believers are the natural structure of this paragraph.

The Repetition of a Phrase Authors may choose to structure their material around a repeated phrase. Notice the repetition of "If we say" in 1 John 1:6, 8, 10.

Questions A small unit or a larger section may be organized with questions. Daniel 12:5-13 consists of two questions (Dan. 12:6, 8). The overall format of Romans 6 and Romans 7 is organized around four questions (these questions come close to being in the category of a repetition of a phrase). They could also be classified as objections. Compare "What shall we say then?" (Rom. 6:1), "What then?" (Rom. 6:15), "What shall we say then?" (Rom. 7:7), and "Has then" (Rom. 7:13). Paul responds to each of these questions with "Certainly not!" (Rom. 6:2, 15; 7:7, 7:13).

Activities The overall structure of a passage may consist of a series of activities. In Psalm 23, the psalmist begins by declaring that the Lord is a Shepherd. Then, he lists the activities of a shepherd. A shepherd makes sheep lie down (Ps. 23:2). He leads beside still waters (Ps. 23:2). He restores (Ps. 23:3). He leads (Ps. 23:3). He comforts (Ps. 23:4). He prepares a table (Ps. 23:5). He anoints (Ps. 23:5). He pursues with goodness and mercy (Ps. 23:6), and He provides a dwelling forever (Ps. 23:6).

Reasons The structure of a passage may be a statement followed by reasons for making such a statement. For example, in 1 Thessalonians 2:1-8, Paul says he was bold to speak the gospel in much conflict (1 Thess. 2:1-2). He then gives two reasons for his action (see "for" at the beginning of verse 3 and the beginning of verse 5). His first reason is that he was convinced his message was from God (1 Thess. 2:3-4). His second reason for boldly proclaiming the gospel was that he was committed to serving others (1 Thess. 2:5-8). Each of these reasons contains a negative and a positive. Paul first tells what his reason was not. Then, he gives his reason (see the outline of this passage below).

Explanations The structure of a passage may be a statement followed by explanations. In 1 Thessalonians 4, Paul exhorts the Thessalonians to not sorrow for departed saints (1 Thess. 4:13). He explains (see "for" at the beginning of verse 14 and again at the beginning of verse 15). His first explanation is that God will raise those who have departed (1 Thess. 4:14). His second explanation is that God will raise departed saints first (1 Thess. 4:15-18).

Subjects Often, an author of Scripture does not use a literary device. In those cases, the structure of the passage is discovered by noticing the change of subject within the literary unit. Sometimes, this change is noticeable, even abrupt; other times, it is subtle and slight. In Psalm 19, the subject shift is dramatic. In the first six verses, the psalmist writes concerning God's work in the world. Abruptly, in verse 7, he switches to God's Word. In verse 12, he turns his attention to people's response to God.

The above list is not exhaustive. For example, a passage may be constructed around a conversation. The point is it is helpful to analyze the natural structure of a literary unit. It is a clue to what is going on in the head of the author.

Additionally, within paragraphs, as well as between paragraphs, there are a number of possible literary relationships (Traina, pp. 50-52). Here is a partial list.

1. Comparison
2. Contrast
3. Repetition (reiteration of the same terms)
4. Continuity (repeated use of similar terms)
5. Continuation
6. Climax
7. Particularization (the movement from the general to the particular)
8. Generalization (the movement from the particular to the general)
9. Introduction
10. Interrogation

Construct an Interpretive Outline

The aim of studying any literary unit of Scripture is to follow the development of the thought through it, the train of thought. Mickelsen states, "To treat material fairly, the modern interpreter must enter into the total train of thought" (Mickelsen, p. 104).

Most passages have major and minor ideas. The object is to

determine the major concepts and identify the minor ones that support them. A simple way to analyze a literary unit to put the major and minor ideas into focus is to outline it. An outline can be extremely effective in understanding what is being said in a passage.

Outlines can also be misleading. For example, many like to alliterate their outlines, which can be a helpful device for clarity, communication, and memory. However, it is possible to get so caught up in producing cute alliteration that the outline misses the ideas in a passage. Even a textual outline or literary analysis outline, as helpful as they may be, can sidetrack the student of Scripture. These kinds of outlines can accurately reflect a passage's content or literary nature, but miss the passage's main idea. An interpretive outline is the best kind of outline for accomplishing that goal. Let me illustrate.

Textual Outline A textual outline uses the words of the text. This type of outline of Matthew 28:18-20 would look like this:

    I. All authority is given to me.
   II. Make disciples of all nations.
      A. Going
      B. Baptizing
      C. Teaching
  III. Lo, I am with you always.

Literary Analysis This kind of outline consists of identifying the literary components of the unit. Such an outline of Matthew 28:18-20 would look like this:

    I. A declaration (Mt. 28:18)
   II. A command (Mt. 28:19-20)
  III. A promise (Mt. 28:20)

Interpretive Outline In both its headings and subheadings, an interpretive outline follows the order and the content of a passage, but it interprets the meaning of the passage. It follows the words of the text, is built on the literary analysis of the text, accurately analyzes the passage, and states the timeless truths of the passage. It interprets it in terms of its significance today. An interpretive outline of Matthew 28:18-20 would be as follows:

I. The authority of the commission is Jesus Christ (Mt. 28:18).
II. The task of the commission is to make disciples (Mt. 28:19-20).
   A. Step 1: Introduction (going and preaching the gospel; Mk. 16:15)
   B. Step 2: Identification (baptizing)
   C. Step 3: Instruction (teaching)
III. The power of the commission is the spiritual presence of Christ (Mt. 28:20)

Each point in the outline must be a complete sentence. A literary unit consists of ideas and not fragments. Therefore, all the points in an outline should be complete sentences to ensure clarity of thought and communication. A speaker may use an alliterated word or phrase outline when speaking, but behind the words should be complete sentences. God did not speak and people do not think in fragments. The Bible consists of concepts and ideas expressed in sentences.

Trace the Logical Development of Thought

Another way to analyze a unit of Scripture is by rewriting the unit in a logical layout. A logical layout simply rewrites the literary unit by sentences in such a way as to reveal the logical relationship between them.

Notice carefully that the focus is on sentences, not verses. Ignore verse divisions. Look for periods. Verses were not in the original text of either the Old Testament or the New Testament. They were added hundreds of years later.

In his commentary on the Gospel of Matthew, Joseph Alexander (1809-1860), whose father was the founder and first professor of Princeton Theological Seminary and who was himself a professor there for 30 years, says that the verse divisions were "the work of a learned printer in the sixteenth century, and not entitled to the least weight in deciding the construction of a sentence or connection of a passage" (Alexander, p. 396). So, look beyond man-made division and discover the natural divisions of Scripture.

The procedure of a logical layout is as follows.

Write out the First Sentence To begin, write the first sentence across the top of a page. In passages with long sentences, like the epistles of Paul, an 8½ x 11 sheet should be turned sideways (landscape) so as to utilize the length of the page.

Ask Questions of Every Other Sentence Then, take the following sentences in order one by one and ask two critical questions: 1) What does this sentence go with? 2) How does it relate to that sentence?

Unit Analysis

1. Ask, "Which sentence does this sentence go with?" The second sentence is obviously somehow related to the first sentence. In fact, as a general rule, each succeeding sentence is probably related to the preceding sentence. However, it is possible that a later sentence could be related to some earlier statement several sentences before it. For example, in 1 Thessalonians 2:1-8, Paul gives several reasons for boldly speaking the gospel. Verses 3 and 5 both begin with the word "for." Perhaps verse 5 is related to verse 4. More than likely, however, it is related to verse 3 in that Paul gives two parallel reasons for his boldness.

2. Ask, "In what way does this sentence go with the one to which it is related?" Determining that two sentences are related is only the first step. The next is to find out how they are related. Basically, there are two possibilities: Either the two sentences are coordinate, that is, they are parallel to each other in thought (1 Thess. 2:3-5 is an illustration of a coordinate relationship), or one sentence is subordinate to the other. In that case, the subordinate sentence would be slightly indented to show its subordinate relationship to the previous sentence.

First Thessalonians 2:1-3 is an illustration. Verse 1 states that they did not come in vain. Verse 2, beginning with the word "but," is a coordinate sentence parallel to verse 1. Verse 3 begins with "for." It is subordinate to those two sentences. Paul is about to explain why he became so bold. Thus, verse 3 should be indented to show its subordinate relationship to verses one and two. Here is a logical layout of 1 Thessalonians 2:1-8.

How To Study The Bible

2:1 For ... know, brethren, that our coming ... was not in vain.
2:2 But ... we were bold ... to speak to you the gospel ....
2:3   For our exhortation did not come....
2:4   But as ... approved ... even so we speak...

2:5   For neither ... did we use....
2:6   Nor did we seek....
2:7   But we were gentle....
2:8   So ... we were well pleased to impart to you....

As a general rule, some words consistently introduce coordinating sentences. Such words as "and" and "but" fall into that category. Some words are used to introduce a subordinate sentence. Such words as "for" and "therefore" are outstanding examples.

Here is an example of a logical layout of Psalm 1:

1:1 Blessed is the man who walks not ... stands ... sits;
1:2 But his delight is ... and ... he meditates ...
1:3   He shall be like a tree planted ... that ...

1:4 The ungodly are not so, but are like the chaff ...
1:5   Therefore, the ungodly shall not ... nor sinners ...
1:6   For the Lord knows ...

To review: Sentences are either coordinate or subordinate in their logical relationship with each other. In tracing the logical development of the thought on paper, coordinate sentences are parallel to each other and subordinate sentences are indented. One other technique: an extra line between sentences indicates a break in thought.

If you have a computer, use it to construct your logical layouts. On a computer, sentences can be moved around with ease.

Summarize the Unit in One Sentence

Analysis is not complete until there is synthesis. Unfortunately, much Bible study consists of analyzing the details of a passage and never putting the details together in a meaningful whole. To succinctly synthesize a literary unit of Scripture, summarize it in one sentence. In the chapter entitled "Correct Interpretation," the single-sentence summary of a whole book was called a message. Actually, each literary unit in a book also has a message that contributes to the overall message of the entire book. To construct the message, a one-sentence summary of the unit, several critical questions need to be asked and answered.

What is the Subject? The subject is the answer to the question, "What is the author talking about?" There are usually several topics in a unit of Scripture. Some are subordinate to others. There is always one subject to which everything is related or by which all is united. "The subject is the organizing or unifying topic within the literary unit" (Johnson, p. 83).

What is the Narrowed Subject? A common pitfall is to assume that a single word is the subject of a unit. A single word is rarely, if ever, by itself a subject. It is tempting to say, for example, that the subject of a particular paragraph is sin, but no one paragraph covers all the aspects of sin, including its definition, its history, its causes, its results, its cure, etc.

The subject of a literary unit needs to be narrowed to a concise phrase so that the subject may be stated as clearly and accurately as possible. The subject of a paragraph is not just sin; it is the result of sin or the solution to sin.

What is the Author saying about the Subject? Once the subject has been narrowed to a concise phrase, it should be completed and made into a complete sentence or a message. If the subject is incomplete, it is nothing more than a fragment, an open-ended phrase.

The subject may be the result of sin. The message could be, "The result of sin is death." Or the narrowed subject could be "the solution of sin." The message would be, "The solution to sin is the blood of Jesus Christ."

The subject of 1 Corinthians 15:1-11 seems to be the gospel. In the opening verse, Paul says, "I declare to you the gospel" (1 Cor. 15:1). Then follows a series of phrases describing the gospel, but beginning at verse 3 through the end of the paragraph, Paul reveals the content of the gospel so that the narrowed subject seems to be "the content of the gospel by which we are saved." The message of the paragraph is "The content of the gospel by which we are saved is that Christ died for our sins and rose from the dead."

Why is the Author saying this here? Just as a verse has a context, which is the paragraph, so the paragraph or other literary units have a context, the larger section of the book in which they are found. To understand the unit's context, the student needs to ask, "Why did the author say that here?" Asking that question will not only reveal the context of the unit but it may also alter the message in the unit. It could even change the subject of the unit itself.

For example, the overall subject of 1 Corinthians 15 is the resurrection from the dead. The first paragraph (1 Cor. 15:1-11) needs to be seen in light of that overall subject. Paul is not talking about the gospel in isolation. He is talking about the gospel as it relates more specifically to the resurrection. When that fact is taken into consideration, it will be seen that the message in 1 Corinthians 15:1-11 is something like "One of the proofs of the resurrection is the gospel by which we are saved, which is that Christ died for our sins and rose from the dead." Seeing 1 Corinthians 15:1-11 in light of the larger context actually changes the subject and message of that paragraph. This is Bible study at its best. It is putting everything in context.

Also, ask questions such as, "How does the message in this passage relate to message of each of the previous units or to the message of each of the following units within the book?" "How does the message here relate to the truth that is being developed?" "How does this message relate to the overall message of the book?"

Summary: The analysis of a literary unit of Scripture studies the parts of the unit to determine its message and to see how that message is developed within the unit.

Unit analysis should be applied to every unit in a book, starting with the first unit and proceeding with each unit to the end of the book. The time it takes to do a unit analysis depends on the size and difficulty of the unit. Some passages are relatively easy and take no more than an hour. Others can take longer. The more you practice this procedure, the easier and faster it will become, even in difficult literary units.

The analysis of each literary unit in the Scripture is the backbone of Bible study. It must be done to thoroughly understand each book as a whole. It must be done to accurately interpret each verse in the Bible. The accurate analysis of each literary unit within the Bible is indispensable to discovering the truth of Scripture that sets us apart from God, the truth that transforms.

Chapter 9

TEXTUAL EXPOSITION

Having done a historical survey, a book synopsis, and a unit analysis, the student is now ready to move to the next level of study, namely, textual exposition. Johnson recommends beginning with a synopsis or summary of the whole book. From the synopsis, analyze the context from which words and phrases are explained (Johnson, p. 11).

The term "text" refers to "the wording of something written" and to "the structure of words in something written." Exposition is the explanation of written material. Thus, textual exposition explains the literary unit's sentences, clauses, phrases, and words. (The word "exegesis" is often used to explain Hebrew or Greek text.) At this stage of study, the details of the literary unit are examined in light of the message of the unit developed through unit analysis.

Needless to say, this is a vital part of the study of the Scripture. "One cannot by-pass the techniques of exegesis and expect to become a profound interpreter of the Bible any more than one can expect to become a great pianist without mastering mechanics of fingering the keyboard" (Traina, p. 18).

At the same time, the danger in textual exposition is that the explanation of grammar becomes an end in itself rather than a means to an end. Traina says, "Grammar is a servant, not a master. In fact, if the use of grammatical terminology is so burdensome that it attracts attention to itself and thereby hinders observation, it should, by all means, be discarded" (Traina, p. 131).

Theoretically, after studying a literary unit as a unit, each sentence within that unit should be analyzed. However, the practical reality is that such a study is more profitable in some passages than others. In narrative material, the sentence simply adds more detail to the narrative, and close scrutiny of the details within it is not as necessary as in didactic material. The most productive place in the Scripture for the close analysis of the details within a sentence is in didactic material, especially in the epistles of Paul, Psalms, and Proverbs. To explain all the details in any passage, systematically follow this procedure.

Look at the Sentence as a Whole

When it comes to reading or studying the Bible, American Christians are so accustomed to thinking in terms of chapters and verses that they sometimes forget that all written material is actually made up of paragraphs and sentences. In the English translation of our Bible, a verse is sometimes only part of the sentence. In other cases, a verse can contain two or more sentences. It is helpful, therefore, to look for the periods and not just the verse numbers. There are three kinds of sentences.

Statement Most sentences in the Bible are either simple or complex statements. Other than the content of the statement itself, not much can be learned from the observation that the sentence is a statement. There are, however, observations about statements that can be helpful. For example, in the New Testament, when a statement begins with "for" (the Greek word gar), it will often be a reason or explanation for what was said in the previous sentence. Paul does this frequently. For example, in Ephesians 5, he says, "Wives, submit to your own husbands as to the Lord" (Eph. 5:22). In the next verse, he says, "For the husband is the head of the wife as also Christ is the head of the church" (Eph. 5:23). The statement in Ephesians 5:23 is the reason for submission, as given in Ephesians 5:22.

Question Questions expect an answer. Even rhetorical questions are asked for the listeners to answer for themselves. Most questions can be answered with a "yes" or a "no." The Greeks had a way of writing that alerted the reader to the answer the author had expected. An English translation does not indicate that literary device, but the context and question usually make the anticipated answer obvious.

An illustration of this is in 1 Corinthians 12:29-30. Paul asks a series of questions: "Are all apostles? Are all prophets? Are all workers of miracles? Do all have the gifts of healings? Do all speak with tongues? Do all interpret?" In the Greek text, there is no doubt that each of these questions expects a "no" answer, but one does not have to know Greek to determine that. It is apparent from just reading the English translation.

Besides the technicality of a New Testament question expecting a yes or no answer, it is also helpful to ask yourself what answer you would expect to a question. By answering that yourself, you may discover that the answer is not the answer you would have expected, or the answer might help you interpret the question.

For example, John 13:36 says, "Simon Peter said to him, 'Lord, where are you going?'" I would expect the answer to be the place where the Lord was headed. However, John 13:36 goes on to say, "Jesus answered him, where I am going, you cannot follow me now, but you should follow me afterward." In other words, John 13:36 is like a small son asking his father, "Daddy, where are you going?" What he means is, "Daddy, can I go with you?" Jesus' answer to Peter's question indicates this is what Peter had in mind. Thus, asking yourself what answer you would expect might help you interpret the question itself.

In his commentary on James, Hodges says that by putting a statement in the form of a question, James is making his readers face what they already know (see his comments on in his commentary on Jas. 2:6).

Command The third type of sentence is a command. Of course, the nature of a command is that someone is exhorting someone else to do something. Some scholars contend that a command in the Greek New Testament can either mean, "Stop doing what you are doing" or "Do not start doing something." Based on this theory, some claim that 1 John 2:15, which says "Love not the world," technically means "Stop loving the world." If that is true, and it should be pointed out that some scholars disagree with this interpretation of a command, it would give insight into the background of the people to whom the author is speaking.

A Scripture command can be universal, occasional, or individual. "You shall not commit adultery" is a universal command given to Israel (Ex. 20:14) and believers in the New Testament (Rom. 13:9). It is also obviously intended to be applied to all men at all times (Rom. 1:28). "Greet one another with a holy kiss" (Rom. 16:16) is an occasional command, meaning when the occasion arises, obey this command. "Go and prepare the Passover for us" (Lk. 22:8) is an individual command Christ gave to Peter and John and is not intended for anyone else at any other time.

Focus on the Parts of a Sentence

Few understood, much less enjoyed, grammar in elementary school. Some did not even have the privilege of studying grammar in elementary school! I must confess that I never really understood grammar until I was forced to take a foreign language in college. However, as painful as it may sound, looking at the parts of a sentence grammatically can be a pleasure, not to mention an aid, in understanding.

Syntax is the way words are put together to form phrases and sentences. It is "a study of thought relations" (Mickelsen, p. 129).

Rather than going into all the technical details concerning the various parts of speech, I would recommend that while looking at the parts of a sentence, you concentrate on four factors—the subject (the doer of the action), the verb (the action), the object (the receiver of the action), and the modifier (a further description of the subject, the verb or the object). In some cases, especially in the long sentences of the apostle Paul, it might be helpful to write the subject, verb, and object on one line and write the modifiers under what they modify.

For example, Ephesians 2:4-7 is one sentence that says, "But God, who is rich in mercy, because of His great love with which

He loved us, even when we were dead in trespasses, made us alive together with Christ (by grace you have been saved), and raised us up together, and made us sit together in the heavenly places in Christ Jesus, that in the ages to come He might show the exceeding riches of His grace in His kindness toward us in Christ Jesus." What is that long, complicated, cumbersome sentence saying to us? To determine that, it would be helpful to analyze the various parts of the sentence.

What is the subject (the doer of the action)? The answer is "God." It is at this point that the complications begin. The rest of the phrases in verse 4 and the first part of verse 5 are descriptive phrases of God. In other words, they are modifiers.

What is the verb (action)? In this case, in this long sentence, there are three verbs. The first is in verse 5 ("made us alive") and the second and third are in verse 6 ("and raised us up ... and made us sit").

What is the object (the receiver of the action)? The object of each of the three verbs is "us." We receive the actions done by God.

What are the modifiers (the further descriptions of the subject, the verb, or the object)? In this sentence, the modifiers are further descriptions of God.

The basic thought of this complicated sentence is that God has made us alive, raised us up, and seated us in heavenly places in Christ. In short, God saved us. That's the basic thought in these four verses. Paul amplifies the God who did this by telling us that He was rich in mercy, He had great love toward us, and that His love was so great He did all of this even when we were dead in trespasses and sins.

A word of caution. Some see more in grammar than is there. For example, the present tense does not always mean continuous action. According to Dana and Mantey, the present tense in Greek can be continuous action, recurring action, or complete action (Dana and Mantey, p. 178). In a conversation, Zane Hodges, who taught Greek for twenty-six years and edited a Greek New Testament, told me that if a point depends on grammar, it is usually wrong because language is not that precise. Therefore, scrutinize such points.

Explain Clauses and Phrases

As we have seen, not all sentences are simple sentences. In fact, most sentences are compound or complex. There is a basic thought, to which is added phrases and clauses that contain additional thoughts. It is helpful and fruitful to analyze the phrases and clauses within a sentence to see the relationship between the different types of clauses as indicated by coordinate and subordinate connectives. The following list contains the most common types of phrases and clauses with the words used to introduce them.

1. Temporal: after, until, when, while, before, then
2. Reason: because, for, since
3. Result: so, then, therefore
4. Purpose: that, so that, in order that
5. Contrast: although, but, much, more, nevertheless, yet
6. Comparison: also, as, likewise, so also
7. Emphatic connectives: indeed, only, even, behold

Traina divides these into four chief categories. 1) chronological connectives: after, as, before, now, then, until, when, while, 2) geographical connectives: where, 3) emphatic connectives: indeed, only, and 4) logical connectives: reason (because, for, since), result (so, then, therefore, thus), purpose (in order that, so that), contrast (although, but, much more, nevertheless, otherwise, yet) comparison (also, ad, just as, likewise, so also), a series of facts (first of all, last of all, or). There may be a connection without the connective being present. The connection is implied (Traina, pp. 41-43). For example, there may be a contrast and the word "but" may not be present.

Decipher Figures of Speech

The plain sense is usually the intended sense of written material. An old adage says, "When the plain sense makes common sense, seek no other sense." Plummer says that when the literal sense makes excellent sense, it is to be preferred (Plummer on 1 Timothy, p. 144). David L. Cooper formulated what he called "The Golden Rule of Interpretation," namely, "When the plain sense of Scripture makes common sense, seek no other sense; therefore, take every word at its primary, ordinary, usual, literal meaning unless the facts of the immediate context, studied in the light of related passages and axiomatic and fundamental truths, indicate clearly otherwise" (Cooper, p. xviii). It would be a grave mistake to interpret the plain sense of Scripture in a figurative sense (spiritual sense) when that is not the Author/author's intended meaning.

Nevertheless, the Bible is loaded with figures of speech. Boonstra says, "Metaphor, simile, and image are central to scriptural language."

He goes on to say, "Such comparisons often capture a truth or a situation or an insight more succinctly than a propositional statement could do" (Boonstra, p. 22).

In all languages, words are used in a literal, metaphorical (figurative), allegorical sense. When authors use figures of speech, they do not intend their words to be taken literally. For example, a teacher says, "Someone is talking." Taken at face value, this is a statement of fact. Someone in the class is speaking. The students, however, recognize that the teacher was not describing the situation in the classroom; she was requesting silence (Johnson, p. 191). Another example is "John is a chicken," which does not mean that John is literally a bird. It means that John is a coward (Johnson, p. 193).

Authors give clues about how they use figures of speech. One way they do that is by using terms of comparison, such as "like," "as," or a genitive construction ("the sword of the Spirit"). Another way is hyperbole (overstatement). For example, Jesus said, "If anyone comes to me and does not hate his father and mother" (Lk. 14:26).

Thus, words have a literal meaning and are often figurative. The literal meaning is the plain meaning. For example, the word "iron" is a specific metal (atomic number 26, atomic weight 55.847). The literal meaning of a word can have an alternative, but still be the plain meaning. The word "iron" can mean something made of iron, such as an appliance used to press fabric or a golf club. That same word may have a figurative (metaphorical) meaning. The expression "he rules with a rod of iron" uses the word "iron" figuratively to convey the idea of a strong rule.

The two most common figures of speech in any literature are

similes and metaphors.

Simile A simile is a comparison utilizing words such as "like" and "as." For example, "Life is like a circus." "His head and hair were white like wool, as white as snow, and His eyes like a flame of fire" (Rev. 1:14). In a simile, two things are similar.

Similes are easy to grasp because that which follows the "like" or "as" is usually commonly understood. To interpret a simile, explain the two things being compared. In His lament over Jerusalem, Jesus cried, "How often I wanted to gather your children together, as a hen gathers her chicks under her wings, but you were not willing" (Mt. 23:37). The care and concern, the provision and the protection that Jesus wanted to extend to the inhabitants of Jerusalem is compared to that which a hen extends to her chicks, only the inhabitants of Jerusalem were not like chicks—they were rebellious.

Metaphor A metaphor is a comparison that omits "like" or "as." For example, "The world is a stage." "The LORD is my rock and my fortress and my deliverer. My God, my strength, in whom I will trust. My shield and the horn of my salvation, my stronghold" (Ps. 18:2). A metaphor is a direct comparison in which the author describes one thing in terms of something else. When Jesus said, "Do not fear, little flock, for it is your Father's good pleasure to give you the kingdom" (Lk. 12:32), He employed the metaphor of "little flock." He is comparing Himself to a shepherd and His followers to sheep. As the shepherd protects and provides for the sheep, so the Lord will care for His own.

Thus the metaphorical meaning, also called figurative meaning, is a comparison in which the primary or ordinary use is applied to something else that is non-literal, but there is a correspondence between the two. To say that a king rules with an iron hand does not mean that he has a hand made of iron. As iron is strong, so he rules with strength.

When Jesus said, "I am the door" (Jn. 10:9), He was using a metaphor. He also used a metaphor when He said, "This is My body" (Lk. 22:19). He intended for this statement to be understood metaphorically rather than literally or physically.

Allegory With metaphors, symbols, and types, the words, people, things, and events are always real and/or historical. In an allegory, the people and events may or may not be historical; they are usually not. The allegorical meaning uses people and events for another meaning. The people and events are usually fictional; they are used as symbols to suggest a deeper or hidden meaning. Furthermore, in an allegory, the literal meaning is the vehicle for a secondary sense. The plain meaning of the text is ignored or denied and the emphasis is placed "entirely on a secondary sense so that the original words or events have little or no significance" (Pentecost, p. 4). The normal meaning is irrelevant and is "replaced by whatever meaning the interpreter gives to the symbols" (Ryrie, *Basic Theology*, p. 110). Pilgrim's Progress is an allegory.

Hyperbole The word "hyperbole" comes from the two Greek words, one for "to throw" and the other for "beyond." Hence, it means to throw beyond excess. Hyperbole is an overstatement, an exaggeration for effect. It is used "when more is said than is literally meant" (Bullinger, p. 423). To say, "I'm so hungry I could eat a horse" is obviously not literally true. It is an exaggeration that conveys the idea of extreme hunger.

Using hyperbole, Jesus said, "If your right eye causes you to sin, pluck it out and cast it from you; for it is more profitable for you that one of your members perish than for your whole body to be cast into hell. And if your right-hand causes you to sin, cut it off and cast it from you; for it is more profitable for you that one of your members perish than for your whole body to be cast into hell" (Mt. 5:29-30).

John used hyperbole when he wrote, "And there are also many other things that Jesus did, which if they were written one by one, I suppose that even the world itself could not contain the books that would be written. Amen" (Jn. 21:25). John painted a graphic picture of how much Jesus did; he was overstating his point to make a point. A complete account would be practically infinite (Westcott).

Personification Personification is portraying an inanimate object as a person. "The mountains and the hills shall break forth into singing before you, and all the trees of the field shall clap their hands" (Isa. 55:12). Mountains do not sing and trees do not clap their hands.

Anthropomorphism An anthropomorphism is using human characteristics to describe God. He is a spirit (Jn. 4:24) and a spirit does not have flesh and bones (Lk. 24:39). So when human characteristics are applied to God, it is anthropomorphism. For example, "Behold, the eye of the LORD is on those who fear Him" (Ps. 33:18). See also "the arm of the Lord" (Isa. 53:1). God is also said to repent (Ex. 32:12; Jer. 18:8; the NKJV says, "relents, regrets"). Does God change His mind, or do these verses describe God from a human point of view?

Figures of Speech

The Name	The Essence	The Significance
Literal	Plain meaning	Used to clearly state something
Simile	Comparison using "like" or "as"	Used to illustrate
Metaphor	Comparison that does not use "like" or "as"	Used to illustrate
Allegory	People and events are symbols for another, hidden meaning	Used to convey a deeper meaning
Hyperbole	Overstatement or exaggeration	Finds hidden meaning
Personification	Portrays an inanimate object as a person	Used for effect
Anthropomorphism	Describing God as having human characteristics	Used for dramatic effect Used to help humans understand God

Explain Customs

A custom is a practice or habit, a culture's usual course of action. Since the cultures and customs in the Bible differ from our own, when we come upon a custom, we often have to investigate it to understand its meaning and significance.

When Boaz redeemed Ruth, he "took off his sandal" (Ruth 4:8) and gave it to the near kinsman. In this case, the Bible explains the custom. Ruth 4:7 says, "Now this was the custom in former times in Israel concerning redeeming and exchanging, to confirm anything: one man took off his sandal and gave it to the other, and this was an attestation in Israel."

At other times, the Bible does not explain the custom, but research both inside and outside of the Bible helps us understand its nature. For example, people in the ancient world often settled disputes and made decisions by casting lots, a custom no longer practiced, at least in the Western world. The Bible nowhere explains to us the mode by which lots were cast. From outside the Bible, we know that the method, at least among some people, was to mark a piece of wood or stone, put the various pieces in a jar or an apron, shake them up and draw one out. To obtain information concerning customs mentioned in the Bible, consult a study Bible, a Bible dictionary, or a commentary.

Define Words

The Study of Words When scholars do a word study of a New Testament word, they begin with the word's etymology and trace its meaning through the classical period of Greek, the Septuagint, the Koine, and its use in the New Testament. That kind of word study can be misleading because what a word meant hundreds of years before the New Testament, perhaps as far back as the classical period (about 800 B.C.), may be totally irrelevant to what that word means in the New Testament itself. The meaning of words changes over time. In a living language, words are born, change, and die.

Let me illustrate. In 1611, the word "let" meant "to hinder." So the King James translators rendered Romans 1:13 "Many times I wanted to come to you, but I was let hitherto." In the 400 years since, the word "let" has completely reversed its meaning so that today it means "to permit" instead of "to hinder." Thus, in the twentieth century, the New King James Version renders Romans 1:13, "I often planned to come to you (but was hindered until now)." That kind of thing happens in Hebrew and Greek. So, when studying a word, be careful.

Nevertheless, there is benefit in word studies. By seeing the meaning of a word at other times and in other contexts, one gets a feel for the field of meaning (the range of possible meanings). Just remember, the word in the passage you are studying has only one or none of those meanings.

The Meanings of Words Furthermore, a word may have any number of meanings. For example, the word "trunk" may mean: 1) the stem of a tree, 2) a large case used for storage, 3) a covered compartment of an automobile, 4) the nose of an elephant, etc.

It is also true that the same word can have different meanings to different people. Winston Churchill talked about a serious misunderstanding because the same word meant two different things to different people. In a meeting of the British and American chiefs of staff, the British delegation proposed to "table" an important resolution. To them, that meant to discuss it immediately. To the Americans, the word meant an indefinite postponement. A heated argument resulted until the committee realized they all wanted the same thing! Ted Pollock, the author of *How to Listen*, says, "The 500 most commonly used English words have more than 2,500 dictionary meanings! Do not believe it? Look up the word 'fix' in a good dictionary."

A dictionary only lists possible meanings. English dictionaries, Hebrew lexicons, Greek lexicons, and grammars give little help concerning how to use a word in a particular sentence. In an article entitled "The New Hermeneutics," Mickelsen writes, "Unfortunately, the best dictionaries and the best grammars give the student little help concerning how to use this information in particular contexts. It is simply not true that a student smart enough to use a lexicon or grammar automatically knows how to use the information in a variety of contextual situations. He needs to know how to relate all his skills to particular passages" (Mickelsen, p. 6).

When a word is used in a sentence, it has only one meaning. The context determines the one meaning of the word that is used in a given passage. Schleiermacher's second canon of interpretation is, "The meaning of any word in a given passage must be determined according to its coexistence with words that surround it" (Hirsch, p. 201). Hirsch adds it is also true that "the sense of a word must determine the senses of the surrounding words" (Hirsch, p. 201).

In some cases, seeing how a word is used outside the immediate context is helpful. Ask how that word is used in the biblical book where it was found. Next, consider how it is used by the same author in another book he wrote. Then, examine how it is used by another author in a parallel passage. After that, see how it is generally used in the New or Old Testament. Remember, regardless of how it is used elsewhere, the meaning of a word is determined by the context where it appears.

Traina calls that one meaning of a word in a sentence a "term," which he defines as "a given word as it is used in a given context" (Traina, p. 34). According to Traina, there are "routine" and "non-routine" terms. "Routine" terms are those whose meaning is immediately obvious and they are not very significant for understanding a passage. "Non-routine" terms fall into three classes: 1) those which are difficult to understand, 2) those which are critical to understanding the passage, and 3) those which express profound concepts (Traina, pp. 34-35).

Terms are also either literal or figurative. Literal terms are those that are used in their primary or usual way. In Genesis 1:12, the term "tree" is literal. "Figurative terms are those which are symbolic and express a secondary idea distinct from their original meaning" (Traina, p. 35). In Romans 11:24, the term "tree" is figurative.

The Use of Words Terms are used in a sentence as verbs, nouns, pronouns, adverbs, adjectives, prepositions, conjunctions, interjections, and articles (Traina, p. 35).

In the final analysis, "Words are building blocks of thought" (Mickelsen, p. 128).

Summary: The exposition of the text of Scripture explains the sentences as a whole and the various parts in them.

If your interpretation of the details explains your summary statement, your understanding of both is the meaning the author intended to communicate. If not, one or the other must be changed.

The procedure described in this chapter should be applied to every literary unit in a book. In fact, as Traina points out, "The exegesis of each unit within a given book should remain tentative until the entire book is studied in order to give full consideration to the broad structural relations, which are frequently so important for proper exposition" (Traina, p. 146).

Commentaries usually concentrate on this type of Bible study. They are a valuable source of information. Unfortunately, they are not always right. Nevertheless, they have their proper place and use. Their place should be secondary to your study, and their use should be to obtain the information you cannot get otherwise or to verify observations you have made. For a more thorough discussion of commentaries, see Appendix III.

Chapter **10**

BOOK SYNTHESIS

All well-written books have a single subject and everything in the book relates to that subject. A book that abruptly shifts to an entirely different subject would be an absurdity. Likewise, biblical books have a single subject.

The approach to Bible study presented thus far is to study the historical situation, survey and summarize the contents of a book, and study the parts of a book, including paragraphs, sentences, and even words. This approach takes a biblical book apart bit by bit. Now, what is needed is for the book to be put back together. It must be seen as a unified whole. Its one subject must be thoroughly established and all the parts, as much as possible, should be seen in relation to that subject.

Imagine studying a sermon the way we study the Bible. The historical circumstances of the sermon would be discussed in detail. The various parts of it would be analyzed, even writing whole books on just the introduction. The style, figures of speech, references to customs, etc., would all be isolated and interpreted. There could be "truth" and value to such a study, but if the whole sermon was not viewed as a unit, the point and purpose of it in the first place would be totally missed.

Likewise, it is not sufficient in Bible study to grasp parts of a book, though that has spiritual value. Instead, the ultimate objective is to understand the entire book, called book synthesis.

The word "synthesis" means "the putting together of parts to form a whole." Thus, book synthesis is viewing the book as the development of a single subject. In synopsis, there is a summary of the parts. In synthesis, there is more concentration on the relationship between the parts and the relationship of the parts to the whole. In other words, in synthesis, the unity of the whole is of the utmost importance.

To obtain the synthesis of any biblical book, follow this procedure.

Step One: Form Sections and Divisions

Begin with Synopsis As has been pointed out, a book of the Bible consists of natural literary units. In "Book Synopsis," these units were isolated and each one was identified with a brief title.

Group Units into Sections The natural literary units of a book, whether they be narratives or paragraphs, now need to be grouped together to form sections. A section is a group of natural literary units with a unifying factor.

For example, Nehemiah 4 is a literary unit and so is chapter 5 and there are at least one or two units in chapter 6. Yet, all three of these units also comprise a section. Each of the units deals with the common factor of opposition. First, there is opposition from without (chapter 4), then from within (chapter 5), and again from without (chapter 6). Thus, these three units, which happen to be chapters, make up a section.

Group Sections into Divisions After grouping all the units of a book into sections, group the sections into divisions. A division is a group of sections with a unifying factor.

For example, there are several sections in Nehemiah 1-6, but all of these can be grouped around a single subject of rebuilding the wall. Thus, Nehemiah 1-6 becomes a division of the book.

There are at least two divisions in every book of the Bible and usually more. Too many divisions, however, would mean that there have not been enough groupings. Seven divisions in a book may be the outside limit.

Step Two: Outline the Book

Having discovered the sections and divisions of a book, it is a relatively easy process to outline the book. The outline is nothing more than arranging the divisions and sections in outline form.

In some biblical books, the author gives a clue to the outline of the book. Revelation 1:19 is the outline of the book of Revelation. Acts 1:8 is a possible outline of the book of Acts. Based on the content of the book, rather than a single verse, another possibility is that the outline of Acts is the acts of Peter and the acts of Paul.

Nehemiah What about the book of Nehemiah? The first six chapters of Nehemiah deal with rebuilding the wall. Chapter 7 contains a registry. In chapters 8-10, a revival breaks out. Chapter 11 deals with the repopulation of the city and, lo and behold, the twelfth chapter records the dedication of the wall built in the first six chapters! If all of that is not confusing enough, the last chapter tells about further restorations that Nehemiah made after an absence from the city for a number of years.

So, what is the outline of Nehemiah? Some divide the book into three parts: rebuilding, revival, and reform. Others divide it into two parts: rebuilding and restoration. Which is correct?

The book opens with Hanani, Nehemiah's brother, returning from Jerusalem (Neh. 1:1-2). Nehemiah asks them, "concerning the Jews who had escaped, who had survived the captivity, and concerning Jerusalem" (Neh. 1:2). They gave Nehemiah a report: "The survivors who are left from the captivity in the province are there in great distress and reproach. The wall of Jerusalem is also broken down, and its gates are burned with fire" (Neh. 1:3). Notice the book opens with two issues: The conditions of the people and the conditions of the city.

There is a clue to the outline of Nehemiah in a repeated statement in the book. Twice in the book, Nehemiah says God put it in his heart to do something about restoration. Nehemiah says, "Then I arose in the night, I and a few men with me; I told no one what my God had put in my heart to do at Jerusalem; nor was there any animal with me, except the one on which I rode" (Neh. 2:12) and "Then my God put it into my heart to gather the nobles, the rulers, and the people, that they might be registered by genealogy. And I found a register of the genealogy of those who had come up in the first return, and found written in it" (Neh. 7:5).

These observations about the book lead to the conclusion that there are two main divisions in the book: rebuilding the wall and restoring the community. If that is the case, the revival is part of the restoration. Based on those observations, Nehemiah can be outlined as follows.

I. Rebuilding of the Wall   1:1-6:19
   A. The Prayer of Nehemiah   1:1-11
   B. The Planning of Nehemiah   2:1-20
   C. The Perspiration of the People   3:1-32
   D. The Persistence of the People   4:1-23
   E. The Prescription of Nehemiah   5:1-19
   F. The Perception of Nehemiah   6:1-19
II. Restoration of the Community   7:1-13:31
   A. The Registry of the People   7:1-73
   B. The Reading of the Law   8:1-18
   C. The Repentance of the People   9:1-38
   D. The Ratification of the Covenant   10:1-27
   E. The Repopulation of the City   11:1-36
   F. The Rededication of the Wall   12:1-47
   G. The Restoration of the People   13:1-31

James Based on the assumption that the outline of James is given in James 1:19, the outline of the book is as follows.

I. Salutation   1:1
II. Prologue   1:2-18
III. Thesis   1:19-20
IV. Be Swift to Hear   1:21-2:26
   A. Hearing is Doing the Word   1:21-25
   B. Hearing is Practicing Mercy   1:26-2:13
   C. Hearing is Producing Works   2:14-26
V. Be Slow to Speak   3:1-18
   A. Teaching and the Tongue   3:1-12
   B. Wisdom and the Tongue   3:13-18
VI. Be Slow to Anger   4:1-5:12
   A. Conflicts   4:1-10
   B. Judging   4:11-12
   C. Planning   4:13-17
   D. Being Treated Unjustly   5:1-12
VII. Epilogue   5:13-20

Step Three: Determine the Message

As has been pointed out, a well-written book has a message. The ultimate aim of synthesis is to determine the message of the book. A message consists of a combination of a narrowed subject and what is said about it. In the case of the entire book, it is the single-sentence summary of the whole book.

Determining the message of a book of the Bible is the most difficult part of Bible study. There are so many variables and so many complexities it is sometimes difficult to determine the exact message. Yet, all of the effort and time it takes to determine the message is well worth it.

As has been explained, the way to determine the message is by asking: What is the subject? What is the narrowed subject? What is the author saying about that subject? What is the message?

What is the Subject? The subject may be stated at the beginning of the book. The opening words of the book of Revelation indicate that the subject of the book is Jesus Christ. It says it is a "revelation of Jesus Christ" (Rev. 1:1).

What is the Narrowed Subject? Jesus Christ is too big of a subject to be covered in one book (Jn. 21:25). As the remainder of the chapter indicates, John narrows his subject to Jesus Christ as Judge (Rev. 1:10-20).

What is the Message? The key to the outline of the book of Revelation is Revelation 1:19. John is told, "Write the things which you have seen, and the things which are, and the things which will take place after this" (Rev. 1:19). Chapter 1 records the things John saw. Chapters 2-3 consist of the things that are, namely, letters to seven churches that are being judged. Chapters 4-22 indicate the things that will take place after this, that is, the world will be judged. Putting all of this together, the message of Revelation is that Jesus Christ is the Judge of the church and the world.

What is the message of Nehemiah? As we have seen from the outline of the book, the bulk of the book is about restoration. Chapter 13 is the conclusion. Even though the wall and the population were restored, there was still another restoration in chapter 13. There had to be continual and perpetual restoration. Thus, the subject of the book is continual restoration with two major divisions. Since it was God who put it in the heart of Nehemiah to do the restoration, the message is God continually restores His people.

What is the message of James? The book opens with a discussion of trials (Jas. 1:2-12) and temptation (Jas. 1:13-18). At the end of the book, James returns to trials (Jas. 5:13). Thus, James's subject is trials. James discusses trials so that believers will develop spiritual maturity and the righteousness of God might be developed in them (Jas. 1:2-4, 1:19). Thus, the narrowed subject is the response to a trial that will produce maturity. The outline of the book is recorded in James 1:19. James says, "Therefore, my beloved brethren, let every man be swift to hear, slow to speak, slow to wrath" (Jas. 1:19-20). The rest of the book seems to be a development of these three commands. Swift to hear is described as doing the word (Jas. 1:22) and James 1:21-2:26 discusses doing the word. Slow to speak is developed in James 3:1-18. Although the word "wrath" does not occur in James 4:1-5:12, that section begins with the theme of conflicts (Jas. 4:1-2) and surely, wrath and anger are involved in not only conflicts but all other subjects in that section. The three commands of James 1:19 are what a believer must do to learn from trials (and avoid temptation), gain the crown of life (Jas. 1:12) and avoid death (Jas. 1:15, 5:19-20). The message is that the way to respond to trial and develop spiritual maturity is to be swift to hear, slow to speak, and slow to wrath.

Other sources may be needed and can definitely aid in determining the subject and the message of a biblical book. Again, a good reference Bible, a Bible dictionary, and commentaries can be valuable.

Whatever it takes, make sure that you do not stop until you find the subject of the book, understand how that subject is developed in the book, and know the message of the book. The first time he read Romans straight through, Dr. James Stalker said, "I began to catch the drift of Paul's thought; or rather, I was caught by it and drawn on. The mighty argument opened and rose like a great work of art before me till, at last, it enclosed me within its perfect proportions. It was a revolutionary experience. I saw for the first time that a book of Scripture is a complete discussion of a single subject; I felt the force of the book as a whole, and I understood the different parts in light of the whole as I had never understood them when reading them by themselves. Thus, to master book after book is to fill the mind with the great thoughts of God" (Gray, pp. 15-16).

Book Synthesis

Step Four: Summarize the Pertinent Data

To really know a biblical book, a person needs to know as much as possible about its five aspects: the author, recipients, message, structure, and purpose. These five parts should have been covered in one or more of the methods applied to the book thus far. Why not write out this pertinent information for future reference? (See my book *The Bible: Book by Book* available at amazon.com or barnesandnoble.com for my version of these five issues on every book of the Bible.)

Author Very often, the author of a biblical book identifies himself, but sometimes he does not. In some cases, there is a uniform and consistent early tradition as to the authorship. In other cases, we are left to speculate. From the information God has allowed us to have, we can conclude that it is not always indispensable for us to know the author of a given book. Yet when that information is available, it can assist in understanding the book. The authorship of the book should have been determined when the historical survey of the book was done.

Recipients One of the most important things a person can know about any biblical book, especially in the New Testament, is who originally received it. This can be as basic as the book's subject or purpose. The setting and the occasion can determine the subject to be discussed and how it will be discussed. Virtually everything we know about the recipients of the various books of the Bible comes from within the books themselves. This data should have been collected during the historical survey.

Message Every book touches on and even discusses many subjects, but the very nature of a book is that it contains one main theme. It would be unthinkable that a university student would be reading a textbook and not at least know the subject of that book, but thousands and even millions of laymen and leaders, preachers, and teachers read the Bible daily without having the faintest idea what the main subject of the book is. Beyond the subject, the student should also know the message of the book. The message of a book is determined by doing a synthesis of that book.

Structure A house has a frame made out of two-by-fours, and a body has a frame made out of bones, so a piece of literary material has a structure. In the case of a book, the structure should be the development of the book's main subject. As all humans have the same structure, at least as compared to animals, and as all ranch-style homes have basically the same structure, books of the same literary type have the same structure. The major types of books in the Bible are as follows.

1. There are history books in the Bible. A history book is a series of narratives, stories, and events with a point or moral. The structure of a historical book is often the chronology of the events.

2. There is a songbook in the Bible. A songbook is a collection of songs. The songbook of the Bible is the book of Psalms. Songbooks are often arranged topically.

3. There are poetry books in the Bible. A poetry book is a collection of poems. The Song of Solomon is a poem. The Psalms are poems. Many of the prophets wrote in Hebrew poetic style. Like songbooks, books of poetry are usually arranged topically.

4. The Bible contains biographical material. Technically, there are no pure biographies in the Bible. Not even the Gospels, which are thought of as biographies of Jesus, are not biographies in the modern sense of the term. By its very nature, a biography discusses all the facts and facets of a person's life, usually chronologically. There are such huge gaps in the Gospels; they are not intended to be pure biographies in the strictest sense of the term. It would be more appropriate to call the Gospels "thematic biographies." Thus, while many biblical books contain much biographical material, no pure biographies exist in the Scripture. The structure of these "thematic biographies" revolves around the subject.

5. There are also letters in the Bible. Actually, there is some discussion about whether or not the "letters" in the New Testament are letters or epistles.

In his book *Light from the Ancient East,* Deissmann says that the discovery of thousands of ancient letters reveals the difference between a letter and an epistle (Deissmann, pp. 149-227). He begins by saying that literature is written to the public and cast in a definite artistic form. A lease or receipts are non-literary. They are records of life but not works of art (Deissmann, p. 148). He goes on to explain that there was a difference between a non-literary letter and epistolary literature in the ancient world. In other words, there is a difference between a real letter and an epistle, which is an artistic letter (Deissmann, p. 149).

Deissmann writes, "What is a letter? A letter is something non-literary, a means of communication between persons who are separate from each other. Confidential and personal in its nature, it is intended only for the person or persons to whom it is addressed and not at all for the public or any kind of publicity. A letter is non-literary, just as much as a lease or a will: There is no essential difference between a letter and an oral dialogue; it might be described as an anticipation of the modern conversation by telephone, and it has been not unfairly called a conversation halved" (Deissmann, p. 228).

What is an epistle? An epistle is an artistic, literary form, a species of literature, just like dialogue, oration, or drama. It has nothing in common with the letter except its form; apart from that, one might venture the paradox that the epistle is the opposite of a real letter. The contents of an epistle are intended for publicity—they aim at interesting "the public" (Deissmann, p. 229).

Deissmann adds that most letters are, at least, partly unintelligible unless the situation of the sender and the recipients are known. Most epistles, however, are intelligible without the author's or recipients' knowledge. He says the letter differs from an epistle as the "halting words of consolation spoken by a father to his childless mother" differs from a "carefully turned funeral oration." He states, "The letter is a piece of life, the epistle is a product of literary art" (Deissmann, p. 230).

The question is, "Are the letters of the New Testament non-literary letters or literary epistles?" Deissmann concludes that both are in the New Testament (Deissmann, p. 233).

He contends that the letters of Paul are not literary; they are real letters, not epistles. "They were written by Paul not for the public and posterity, but for the persons to whom they are addressed." Philemon is the clearest example of a letter (Deissmann, p. 234). Paul's letters were "raised to the dignity of literature afterward" and "still later they became sacred literature," but originally, Paul's writings were non-literary letters (Deissmann, p. 240). He also calls 2 John and 3 John "real letters" (Deissmann, p. 241), insisting that 3 John is "a private note."

Deissmann claims that James, Peter, and Jude are literary epistles. He says, "A glance at the 'addressees' shows that these are not real letters." In other words, these were not letters addressed to a particular person or location. A letter addressed to "the twelve tribes which are scattered abroad" would be "simply undeliverable." Therefore, these three are "pamphlets" (Deissmann, p. 242). He calls "the letter-like touches" of these "merely decorative" (Deissmann, p. 243). According to Deissmann, Revelation is "strictly speaking an epistle." The letters to the seven churches are "not real letters." They were written "with an eye to the whole" and intended for all the churches (Deissmann, p. 244). First John has none of the "special characters of an epistle and is even less like a letter. It is a religious "diatribe, in which Christian meditations are loosely strung together" (Deissmann, p. 244).

While some of Deissmann's conclusions are misguided (1 John is not a diatribe), he makes a legitimate point. The discovery of ancient letters reveals the format of a letter. The distinction between a letter and an epistle is helpful. Nevertheless, Deissmann goes too far when he suggests that Paul's writings were not for the public and posterity but only for the persons to whom they are addressed. Paul said, "I charge you by the Lord that this epistle be read to all the holy brethren" (1 Thess. 5:27) and "Now when this epistle is read among you, see that it is read also in the church of the Laodiceans and that you likewise read the epistle from Laodicea" (Col. 4:16). As Lown says,

"While this delineation has some validity, it should not be imposed on the NT writings mechanically or indiscriminately" (J. S. Lown, in the article on "Epistle" in ISBE, vol., II, p. 124).

A more accurate conclusion would be to say that some books of the New Testament follow the *format of an ancient letter* (not exactly in every case), which are *intended for public use* and which *contain "literary" elements.*

A modern personal letter has a standard format. The date is placed in the upper right-hand corner. The salutation ("Dear John") appears on the left-hand side of the page, followed by the body of the letter. The name of the author appears at the end of the letter. Likewise, an ancient letter also had a standard format, which consisted of six parts: The salutation (which included an identification of the author and recipients as well as a greeting), a thanksgiving, a prayer, the body of the letter, personal greetings, and a benediction.

This phenomenon explains the structure of the epistles of the New Testament. The New Testament authors utilized the letter's basic format, but they also "Christianized" them. For example, they used a Christian greeting instead of a pagan greeting and they often expanded the "thanksgiving" and "prayer," dropping clues about what was coming. Noting changes in the standard format is a fruitful exercise. (See J. S. Lown, in the article on "Epistle" in ISBE, vol., II, pp. 122-125, esp., his discussion on Paul's form, p. 124.)

Paul's epistles follow the format of an ancient letter. Each contains a salutation, a thanksgiving, a prayer, the body of the letter, personal greetings, and a benediction. Any change in his format would be significant, which is what happens in Galatians. In Galatians, Paul omits the thanksgiving. He was not thankful for those who turned away to a different gospel (Gal. 1:6). Such a significant omission would have been noticed immediately.

Sigmund Freud and Carl Jung met in 1907. They struck up a friendship that lasted for six years. Since Freud lived in Vienna and Jung lived in Zurich, much of their friendship was by correspondence. They regularly wrote to each other. At that time, letterwriting was governed by extremes of etiquette. Freud addressed his letters with the usual professional salutation of "Dear Friend and Colleague." When Freud wanted to move their relationship from professional to more personal, he changed the salutation in a letter from the usual professional one to the more intimate "Dear Friend." According to his biographer, "Jung noticed the change immediately" (Bair, Jung, p. 131).

The "letter" aspect of some of the books of the New Testament not only gives them a format, but it also gives them a personal touch and a natural flow. In his commentary on 1 Timothy, Plummer argues that 1 Timothy is a real letter, not a theological or controversial treatise because the thoughts "follow one another in an order which is quite natural, but which has little plan or arrangement" (Plummer, p. 164). It would be more accurate to say that 1 Timothy has a plan and the natural flow of a letter.

At the same time, the "letters" of the New Testament were intended for a wider audience than the ones to whom they are addressed. Moreover, there are portions that are, if not literary, at least border on literary (1 Cor. 13). As an essay, a treatise, or a formal systematic presentation is used to convince, so the "letters" of the New Treatment are designed to convict, convince, and convert.

Purpose Knowing why something was written is indispensable to understanding what is written. The purpose is one of the most important and yet one of the most neglected aspects of Bible study. Students should constantly ask, "Why did the author say this and why did he say it here?" No book of the Bible should be preached or taught until the speaker has determined why this book was written and what the author was trying to accomplish.

Summary: Book synthesis puts the parts of a book of the Bible together to determine its message. A Biblicist should be a synthesist.

The whole consists of parts in relationship. The whole is not just the sum of the parts; an auto parts store is not a car. Each book of the Bible is like a car, the combination of many parts in a meaningful whole. Breaking the Bible into small segments is as misleading as plucking a piece of a jigsaw puzzle from the box and studying it. One might learn everything about the piece, yet little of the whole picture. The full picture is appreciated only after all the pieces are put together. Students of the Scriptures should not be satisfied with a study of any book until they have an understanding of that whole.

Once the whole is obtained, why not write out your conclusions? Writing out this data will clarify it in your mind and preserve it for future use. The following are illustrations of synthesis for Nehemiah and James.

Book Synthesis

NEHEMIAH

In the Hebrew canon, Ezra and Nehemiah are one book. They were once called 1 and 2 Ezra. Jerome first called the second book Nehemiah. The present names of both books were first given in the Geneva Bible (1560).

Author Nehemiah 1:1 says that Nehemiah wrote the book. He composed the book, but he undoubtedly compiled parts of it. Nehemiah 7:5-73 is almost identical to Ezra 2:1-70. Both lists may have been taken from the same document.

Recipients Nehemiah served under Artaxerxes I of Persia, who reigned from 464 to 423 BC (Neh. 2:1). He left Persia in the twentieth year of Artaxerxes, which was 445 BC (Neh. 2:1). He returned to Persia in the thirty-second year of Artaxerxes, that is, 432 BC (Neh. 13:6). Later, he returned to Jerusalem, perhaps around 425 BC. He probably wrote the book around that time. The recipients of the book, the remnant in Jerusalem after the captivity, experienced the events of the book. Nehemiah was not written to correct some needs in the people but to remind them what God had done among them.

Message The subject of the book of Nehemiah is continual restoration. He rebuilt the wall, repopulated the city, and spiritually restored the people twice. The message of the book is God continually restores.

Structure The key to the structure is in Nehemiah 2:12 and 7:5. These verses reveal that God put it in Nehemiah's heart to do two things: rebuild the wall and restore the population of Jerusalem. Thus, the book should be divided into two parts: rebuilding the wall (chapters 1-6) and restoring the city (chapters 7-13). Some divide the book into three parts: rebuilding (chapters 1-7), revival (chapters 8-10), restoration (chapters 11-13). While that division may reflect the content, the structural clues given in 2:12 and 7:5 indicate that it is better to divide the book into two parts and consider the revival part of the restoration. The book can be outlined as follows:

I. The Rebuilding of the Wall — Chapters 1-6
   A. The Prayer — Chapter 1
   B. The Planning — Chapter 2
   C. The Perspiration — Chapter 3
   D. The Persistence — Chapter 4
   E. The Prescription — Chapter 5
   F. The Perception — Chapter 6

II. The Restoration of the Community — Chapters 7-13
   A. The Registry — Chapter 7
   B. The Revival — Chapter 8-10
   C. The Repopulation — Chapter 11
   D. The Dedication — Chapter 12
   E. The Restoration — Chapter 13

Purpose The Purpose of Nehemiah is to show that God not only restores, He repeatedly, constantly, and continually restores.

Summary: Nehemiah wrote to the remnant who rebuilt the wall to show how God used him to rebuild the wall, repopulate Jerusalem, and continually restore the people.

JAMES

Luther called the book of James "a right strawy epistle," presumably referring to the stubble in 1 Corinthians 3:12. He accused it of "having no true evangelical character." Luther was mistaken (Jas. 2:23).

Author The author of this epistle identifies himself as James and calls himself a servant (Jas. 1:1) and a teacher (Jas. 3:1). Beyond that, the epistle itself reveals nothing about the author. That fact seems to indicate that he was well-known at the time.

Who was James? There were three prominent men named James in the New Testament. The first was James, the son of Zebedee, the older brother of the apostle John (Mt. 10:2). His martyrdom by AD 44 makes it unlikely that he was the author of this epistle (Acts 12:2). The second was James, the son of Alphaeus, the brother of Matthew (Mt. 10:3). Apart from being listed with the other disciples this James is comparatively obscure. Thus, it is doubtful that he is the authoritative figure behind this epistle. The third was James, the son of Joseph, the half-brother of Jesus Christ (Mt. 13:55). At first, he did not believe (Jn. 7:5), but after the Lord appeared to him (1 Cor. 15:7), he became a believer (Acts 1:14) and one of the pillars at Jerusalem (Acts 12:7; 15:3; 21:18; Gal. 2:12-19).

James, the son of Joseph, best fits the evidence as the author of this epistle: 1) There is no title indicating he was well known. 2) It was written to scattered Jewish Christians. James, the half-brother of Jesus, was the leader of the Jerusalem church. When the early Jewish believers scattered, he was the most likely to write to them. 3) The vocabulary of this book resembles the vocabulary of James' speech in Acts 15. 4) Tradition says that James, the half-brother of Jesus, was the author, and that tradition was not questioned until the Reformation when Luther questioned the whole epistle.

Recipients According to Josephus, James was martyred in AD 62. Those who accept him as the author have proposed dates for his writing this epistle from AD 45 to the end of his life. Many, if not most, believe it was written early. One of the main reasons for that is that James uses the word "synagogue" (see "assembly" in 2:2), as well as the word "church" (5:14), indicating that these believers were still meeting in the synagogue. James was probably written about AD 45, making it either the first book or one of the first books written in the New Testament collection.

The recipients were Jewish (Jas. 1:1) Christians (see "brethren" throughout, except Jas. 5:1-6). The book is addressed to "the twelve tribes which are scattered abroad." This is probably a reference to the Jewish Christians who were scattered abroad because of the persecution in Acts 8:4 (Acts 9:2; 11:19). If so, then they were in Syria (Acts 11:19). From the book, it is obvious that these Jewish Christians were still meeting in synagogues (Jas. 2:2) and had elders (Jas. 5:14). Strangers sometimes attended their meetings (Jas. 2:2-4). While some among them were rich (Jas. 1:10), even traveling traders (Jas. 4:13 ff.), the majority were probably poor (Jas. 1:9; 2:6; 5:1-6).

The original recipients of James were experiencing various kinds of trials. Unsaved, rich men were oppressing them by hauling them before the courts (Jas. 2:6-7) and wrongfully withholding their wages (Jas. 5:4). Perhaps religious persecution was involved (Jas.

2:7). Furthermore, these believers were having trouble among themselves. They had disagreements, ambitions, and strife (Jas. 3:13-18; 4:1, 2, 11). Some were weak from sickness (Jas. 5:13), probably as a result of God's chastening. To make matters worse, they were not enduring their trials with joy and submission. They were being partial (Jas. 2:1-13). Many were trying to give advice, assuming the role of teacher (Jas. 3:1). They had bitter jealousy and strife in their heart (Jas. 3:14) causing them to misuse the tongue to abuse one another (Jas. 3:9, 10), arguing with one another (Jas. 4:1), speaking against one another (Jas. 4:11), and groaning against one another (Jas. 5:9). They were lusting after things (Jas. 4:2) and were not praying properly (Jas. 4:4), acting as if they were self-sufficient, they did not consider the will of God (Jas. 4:13, 16). Since they needed to take oaths (Jas. 5:12), it appears that they were not completely honest with each other.

Message The subject of James is trials. He begins by discussing trials and concludes by returning to the subject of trials. He develops various other subjects that, one way or another, relate to the subject of trials. The message is that the way to respond to trials to develop spiritual maturity is to be swift to hear, slow to speak, and slow to wrath.

Structure Technically, James is not a letter. It contains none of the features of an ancient letter except for the salutation. Whatever the literary form, the structure seems to be summarized in James 1:19. A suggested outline is as follows:

Salutation	1:1
Prologue	1:2-18
Theme	1:19-20
I. Be Swift to Hear	1:21-2:26
A. Hearing is doing the word	1:21-25
B. Hearing is practicing mercy	1:26-2:13
C. Hearing is producing works	2:14-26
II. Be Slow to Speak	3:1-18
A. Inconsistent use of the tongue	3:1-12
B. Godly wisdom and the tongue	3:13-18
III. Be Slow to Anger	4:1-5:12
A. The cause of conflict	4:1-6
B. The cure for conflict	4:7-5:12
Epilogue	5:13-20

Purpose The purpose of James was to exhort Christians to properly respond to trials and to warn them about the dangers in the middle of a trials. He exhorts them to trust God and endure. If they were to be mature, they must be swift to hear, slow to speak, and slow to wrath. He warns them of the dangers of temptation (Jas. 1:13-18), a lack of works (Jas. 1:21-2:28), prejudice (Jas. 2:1-12), judging one another (Jas. 4:11-12), leaving God out of business plans (Jas. 4:13-17), and even bitterness (Jas. 5:6-12).

Summary: James, the half-brother of Jesus Christ, wrote to Jewish Christians outside Palestine who were going through various trials to exhort them to respond properly and warned them about the dangers they faced in the process.

Chapter 11

TOPICAL STUDY

God wrote His book by books, so we should study the Scripture by books. That does not mean, however, that there are no other legitimate methods of studying the Scripture. Other methods are not only legitimate but are also essential in finding truth unto godliness. While there are major subjects in each book, and those subjects are indeed major, there are also major subjects in the Bible that do not constitute the subject of a book of the Bible. For example, the doctrine of the Trinity is the foundation of biblical Christianity. Indeed, without it, there would be no Christianity! Yet, no book of the Bible has as its subject the Trinity. In fact, no paragraph has the Trinity as its subject. Instead, that truth is recorded and revealed throughout the Scripture in various ways.

Thus, there are major topics that a book or unit analysis of the Scripture would never systematically study. One must apply a topical study to the Bible to understand these truths. A topical study is studying a subject through a book or the Bible to determine what the Scripture teaches about it.

There are hundreds of major and minor topics in the Bible. The topics that should be studied are those the Bible addresses and which contribute to the overall thrust of Scripture. For example, some legitimate biblical topics worthy of study would be God, man, salvation, church, prophecy, family, the believer's relationship to government, prayer, etc. Through the centuries, many of these major topics have been dealt with repeatedly and have become called areas of theology. In a sense, the study of theology is nothing more than the study of particular topics of the Bible. There are topics, however, outside the standard framework of theology. These are also legitimate topics for study.

At the same time, some topics would not be legitimate topics for study. I once heard a preacher speak on "Nights of the Bible." While obviously, the Bible refers to "night" in several places, it never addresses the topic of nights. To do a topical study of nights would be artificial and superficial at best.

Assuming that you have chosen an appropriate topic to study, follow this procedure to do it properly.

List All of the References on that Subject

The Procedure To begin a topical study, determine all the references to that topic. If you are studying a topic within a book, all the references within that book must be assembled. If you are studying that same topic throughout the Bible, all the references must be amassed.

Let me illustrate. The subject of Satan comes up repeatedly in the book of 2 Corinthians. It would be possible to do a topical study of Satan, limiting the discussion to just 2 Corinthians. On the other hand, there are repeated references to Satan throughout the Bible. To do a thorough study of Satan would necessitate considering all of the references to him in all of the books of the Bible.

To obtain all the references for any topic, either in a single

Topical Study

book or in the entire Bible, you must use a concordance. An exhaustive concordance lists all the references of the words of the Bible. Strong's Concordance is the exhaustive concordance for the King James Version of the Bible. Though not quite as exhaustive as Strong's, Young's Concordance is very helpful. Modern translations have also produced concordances for their version. The concordance for the New King James is entitled *The Complete Concordance of the Bible*. If you have a Bible on your computer, you can search for a word that will give you all the references to that word in that version of the Bible.

The Problems There are several problems with using any English concordance. In the first place, some English concordances should be avoided altogether. For a topical study, the concordance in the back of your Bible should not be used for the simple reason that it is not complete or exhaustive.

The other major problem with using an English concordance is that a particular word may have multiple translations. Technically, the study of a word or topic should begin by looking up that word or topic in a Hebrew or Greek concordance. For those who do not know the original languages, that becomes difficult, though not impossible. Both Strong's and Young's Concordances can give you that information even if you do not know Greek or Hebrew. Strong uses a numbering system whereby each Hebrew or Greek word has a number. The meaning of a Hebrew or Greek word can be determined by looking up that number in the back of the book. Young lists English, Hebrew, and Greek words and all the occurrences of that particular English word. Keep in mind that both Strong and Young are concordances of the King James Version.

Make sure that you have all the translations of the word you wish to study. As mentioned before, some words or topics have more than one translation. In the study of the topic of faith, you would obviously look up that word in a concordance, but the verb is translated "believe." So, to obtain all of the references on the subject of faith, you would have to look up "believe" as well as "faith." "Believe" is also sometimes translated "trust." That compounds the process.

To further complicate this type of study, there are cases where the same English word translates several different words. For example, there is only one word for "love" in English, whereas in the Greek New Testament, there are two different words for "love." (Actually, there are four different words for love in the Greek language of the first century. Only two occur in the New Testament.) So, when you have all the references to a word, make sure that you are dealing with the same Greek or Hebrew word.

Make sure you have all the synonyms of the word you are studying. In some cases, several different words refer to the same topic. While there might be shades of differences among synonyms, a thorough study of a topic would include the use of synonyms. For example, the New Testament uses several words with slightly different meanings to describe anger. Anger, wrath, and bitterness are all in this category. A thorough investigation of anger would include looking up all the references to all of these words.

Make sure you have references where the subject is not named directly or indirectly. To make the life of a Bible student interesting, the Bible sometimes talks about a subject and never names it!

The Bible has much to say about conscience, but the word never occurs in the Old Testament. There are references to "conscience" in the New Testament where the word "conscience" is not used. In most of these cases, another word is used, such as "heart." First John 3:20 is an outstanding example. In studying the baptism of the Holy Spirit, you would automatically look up the word "baptism" in a concordance. If that were all you did, you would miss Act 8, which never uses the term "baptism of the Holy Spirit," but many feel Act 8 refers to that subject.

Doing a topical study is not as easy as it may first appear. For starters, students must be certain they have all the references to that subject in the book they are studying or in the Bible.

Study Each Passage in Context

The Problem If the first great danger of a topical Bible study is that you will not find all of the references, the second is that you will be tempted to make superficial observations and not understand the context. I am skeptical in my study when I look at a verse I have not studied in its natural literary unit. Most amateur Bible students begin with word studies or topical studies, but a topical study is a very advanced stage of Bible study. It assumes you understand the context of every reference!

I realize that what I am saying may be overwhelming to some. At the same time, it is vitally important that you do not make snap judgments based on superficial observations about particular references to any topic.

The Procedure Students of the Word doing a topical study should do at least a brief unit study of each passage where the topic is mentioned to guarantee that they are studying that topic within the context of the passage. Ideally, the entire book needs to be studied because the basic context is the book.

Organize the Results of the Study

Assuming that every reference has been found and has been studied in context, the result of the study needs to be organized in some fashion.

Natural to the Topic The organization of the topic may naturally fall into place and suggest itself during the study. A way to organize the material concerning the Tabernacle, for instance, is around the various items of furniture. That organizational principle is intrinsic to and unique to the Tabernacle itself. The division of the subject of the family would include husband, wife, father, mother, children, and in-laws.

Types or Kinds In some subjects, "types" or "kinds" may be organizational factors. Such might be the case in the topic of prayer. Prayer can be divided into praise, thanksgiving, confession, petition, intercession, and supplication.

Traditional Divisions If the topic is a standard topic of theology, a recognized division already exists. For example, the topic of Christ is divided into the person and work of Christ. The doctrine of man is traditionally divided into two parts: dignity and depravity.

Whatever organizational principle is used, the point is that the result of the study ought to be organized.

Determine the Major Passages

Many topics of the Scripture have one passage that discusses that topic more extensively than others. That becomes "the major" passage for that topic. For example, Ephesians 5 is the major passage in the New Testament on the topic of the husband/wife relationship.

When I studied theology under Dr. Charles Ryrie at Dallas Seminary, he had us memorize the "central passage" for many of the major points of doctrine. That has been extremely helpful in the years since.

Determine the Lessons and Principles

After the material on the topic is organized and the major passages determined, the major lessons and principles should be clearly stated. Each lesson or principle should be stated in a complete sentence.

Summary: The topics of the Bible, as well as the books of the Bible, should be studied, but a topical study can be, and often is, complicated and difficult, yet it is necessary and rewarding.

Chapter 12

BIOGRAPHICAL STUDY

God delights in pouring truth into people, who become examples from whom we learn. If the biographical data were taken out of the Bible, that large book would be reduced to a booklet. Studying the people of the Bible is a legitimate and beneficial way to study the Scriptures to gain spiritual truth.

In a sense, a biographical study is a type of topical study. By definition, a biographical study examines people to determine the principles that govern their lives. To do a biographical study, follow these steps.

Collect all the References

Like a topical study, the biographical study begins by collecting all the references to that particular person, either in a specific book or in the Bible as a whole. To obtain this information, look up a person's name in an exhaustive concordance. However, as in a topical study, pitfalls must be avoided.

All the Names Be sure to include all of the person's names. Some people in the Scriptures have more than one name. To find all of the references to any one person, all of his names and all of the references to those names must be considered. For example, a man in the Bible named Simon later had his name changed to Peter. In studying Paul, remember his hebrew name was Saul.

All the Same Person Do not include too many people in the list. Just as there are many people by the same name today, there are cases in the Bible where more than one person has the same name. For example, there are at least four men in the New Testament named James and no telling how many named John. There is a man named Saul, who became king in the Old Testament, and a man named Saul, who became an apostle in the New Testament. The list runs on and on.

All the References Be sure to obtain all the references for each person. Again, like the topical study, some passages mention a person but do not mention his name. Mark never referred to himself by name in his Gospel, but many feel that there are veiled references to him. John never refers to himself directly in the fourth Gospel; however, the reference to the one "whom Jesus loved" (Jn. 13:23) is no doubt a reference to him.

Study Each Passage in Context

The cardinal rule of all Bible study is context. It is no different when studying an individual in the Bible. Perhaps the context in a biography is not as critical as in some topical studies, but it is nonetheless important. Nothing in the Bible should be taken out of context.

The unit study should be applied to every passage where the person's name or a reference to him or her appears to make sure the context is not violated.

Biographical Study

Reconstruct the Person's Life

Unlike topics, people always have a history and a chronology. It is not always possible to construct a complete history or chronology of the people in the Bible, but as much as possible, that should be done. If the information is available, the reconstruction should begin with the person's birth, cover all of the events in the person's life in chronological order and conclude with their death. Unfortunately, that is not always possible because the data is lacking.

Organize the Person's Life

The reconstruction of a person's life may be sufficient to organize it. Chronology would be excellent for Moses. He was forty years in Egypt, forty years in the desert, and forty years in the wilderness. However, there are cases when a simple reconstruction is not the best means of organization. Other types of organizations may be better for any particular person. In the case of Peter, perhaps, a better organizational principle would be the various crises of his life, including his call to discipleship, his commission, his collapse, his confession, and the commencement of his ministry.

Noting the positions of David's life captures it. He was a shepherd, a musician, a fugitive, and a king.

Another way to organize an individual's life is around the lessons learned from that person.

Determine the Lessons and Principles

After all the data is collected, the spiritual truth(s) from the person's life should be stated as simply and clearly as possible. Every individual has at least one "life message." These messages may be negative, as in the case of King Saul. Hopefully, most of the lessons we learn from the people in the Bible will be positive. Barnabas is an example of an encourager. Warren Wiersbe recommends building the character's life around one main truth. He says that for Jonah, it might be prejudice (*Prokope*, vol. III, no. 2, March-April 1986).

Summary: The people of the Bible should be studied so that we can emulate the godly virtues of their lives and avoid the pitfalls of their vices.

After your personal study is complete, you might want to see what others have learned from studying the various people of the Bible. Studies of people can be found in Bible dictionaries and books on Bible characters, such as *Bible Characters* by Alexander Whyte. Wiersbe highly recommends *The Representative Men and Women of the Bible* by George Matheson.

PART III

MEDITATING ON SPIRITUAL TRUTH

Chapter 13

MEDITATING ON THE EVALUATION OF TRUTH

If there is any Bible study method mentioned in the Bible itself, it is meditation. God wants His children to think about His Word. Consider:

- "This Book of the Law shall not depart from your mouth, but you shall meditate in it day and night, that you may observe to do according to all that is written in it. For then you will make your way prosperous, and then you will have good success" (Josh. 1:8).
- "But his delight is in the law of the Lord, and in His law, he meditates day and night" (Ps. 1:2).
- "When I remember you on my bed, I meditate on You in the night watches" (Ps. 63:6).
- "I will also meditate on all Your work, and talk of Your deeds" (Ps. 77:12).
- "I will meditate on Your precepts, and contemplate Your ways" (Ps. 119:15).
- "Princes also sit and speak against me, but Your servant meditates on Your statutes" (Ps. 119:23).
- "My hands also will lift up Your commandments, which I love, and I will meditate on Your statues" (Ps. 119:48).
- "Let the proud be ashamed, for they treated me wrongfully with falsehood; but I will meditate on Your precepts" (Ps. 119:78).
- "My eyes are awake through the night watches, that I may meditate on Your Word" (Ps. 119:148)

- "I remember the days of old; I meditate on all Your works; I muse on the work of Your hands" (Ps. 143:5).
- "Finally, brethren, whatever things are true, whatever things are noble, whatever things are just, whatever things are pure, whatever things are lovely, whatever things are of good report, if there is any virtue and if there is anything praiseworthy—meditate on these things" (Phil. 4:8).
- "But he who looks into the perfect law of liberty and continues in it, and is not a forgetful hearer but a doer of the work, this one will be blessed in what he does" (Jas. 1:25). (The Greek word for "continues" means "to continue beside," perhaps a reference to meditation.)

What is meditation? There are two Hebrew words translated "meditate." One means "moan, growl, meditate, muse" (Jos. 1:8; Ps. 1:2; 63:6; 77:12; 143:5). It is to ponder, imagine, and even study. The other means "to muse, meditate upon, study" (Ps. 119:15, 23, 48, 78, 148). Biblical meditation is pondering over God's Word (Jos. 1:8; Ps. 1:2; 119:12, 23, 48, 78, 148), His works in His Word (Ps. 143:5), and His ways as gleaned from His Word (Ps. 119:15).

Biblical meditation is not Eastern meditation. Eastern meditation is attempting to empty the mind. Biblical meditation is filling the mind with God's Word and ways.

Biblical meditation is not the "Christian" meditation of the Classical Disciplines. In the tradition of the "Devotional Masters," meditation is contemplation that is described as "an encounter between a person and God" (Foster, p. 3). Foster says, "Christian meditation, very simply, is the ability to hear God's voice and obey his word" (Foster, p. 17). He also says, "What happens in meditation is that we create the emotional and spiritual space which allows Christ to construct an inner sanctuary in the heart" (Foster, p. 20) and "it catapults us into a divine-humans encounter" (Foster, p. 23). That is pouring too much into the concept. Biblical meditation is pondering, thinking through, and studying God's Word. There may (or may not) be an emotional reaction and the result may (or may not) be obedience, but biblical meditation is simply thinking through what God says.

The problem for modern Americans is that meditation is a lost art. From the moment we get up in the morning until we go to bed at night, our minds are bombarded with a million messages from myriad directions. We read the paper, listen to the radio, see billboards, talk to our friends, talk on our cell phones, watch TV, spend hours in front of a computer, etc. Our minds are saturated. What we have lost is the practice of meditating on Scripture.

The experts tell us that no one can concentrate on anything for more than seven seconds. We refer to this phenomenon as "our minds wandering." The issue is, to what does your mind wander? If you are young and in love, no matter what you are doing, you are thinking about your beloved. Avid sports fans never have their team very far out of mind. The art of meditation is nothing more than letting your mind wander to the Scripture instead of something else.

The question is, "What do people think about when they meditate on the Scripture?" They think about the Scripture, but what does that mean? Meditating on the Scripture can be divided into two categories. The first is "evaluation," and the second is "application." In simple terms, meditation means thinking about the Scripture in relation to the Scripture (evaluation) or the Scripture in relation to life (application). Evaluation answers the question, "Where does this truth fit in the Bible?" Application is concerned with the question, "How does this truth fit in my life?" The first of these will be discussed in this chapter, and the second will be discussed in the next chapter.

When people think about the Scripture in terms of the Scripture itself, they evaluate what they read so as to interpret it in light of the whole of Scripture. That is evaluation. There are levels of evaluating a truth from the Scripture.

The Book of the Bible

The Principle All Bible study should be rooted in the immediate contextual analysis of a passage. No statement should be interpreted apart from its immediate context, but having done that, the next step is to evaluate the truth mined from a passage in light of the book in which it is found. The question needs to be asked, "How does this truth fit, correlate, or relate to other truths in this biblical book?"

An Illustration For example, 1 John 3:9 says, "Whoever has been born of God does not sin, for His seed remains in him; and he cannot sin, because he has been born of God." Does that verse mean that one born of God is sinless? The verse plainly says, "Whoever has been born of God does not sin ... and he cannot sin." That verse seems to say that anyone born of God does not sin. The problem is that those who have trusted Jesus Christ and are honest with their hearts know this is not true. What does John mean by the statement of 1 John 3:9?

The one thing John could not possibly mean is that a person is sinless. That can be easily determined by simply asking the question, "What does John say in 1 John on the subject of sin in the life of believers?" One answer is in 1 John 1:8, "If we say we have no sin, we deceive ourselves, and the truth is not in us," or again in 1 John 1:10 when he writes, "If we say that we have not sinned, we make Him a liar, and His word is not in us." Whatever 1 John 3:9 means, it cannot mean sinless perfection. The one who penned the words made that clear.

The purpose of bringing up this verse is not to solve the difficult problem of explaining 1 John 3:9. It is to illustrate that any given verse in the Bible must be evaluated in light of its immediate context and the context of the book in which it appears. That's part of meditation.

By the way, the most common solution to 1 John 3:9 is to say that "does not sin" is in the present tense; therefore, the verse means that a person born again does not *practice* sin. According to this interpretation, when John says, "cannot sin," he means cannot practice sin. That interpretation pours too much into the present tense. More recent commentaries on 1 John have rejected that explanation as the solution to the verse.

A second possible solution is to suggest that the latter part of the verse explains the first. In 1 John 3:9, the apostle wrote, "For His seed remains in him, and he cannot sin, because he has been born of God." "His seed" is a reference to the divine nature within the believer. The new nature, His seed, does not sin. This interpretation is to be preferred, but whatever interpretation is correct, 1 John 3:9 is not teaching sinless perfection. That is certain because of the statements in 1 John 1:8, 10.

Meditation on a verse in light of the book in which it occurs will prevent a person from reaching an erroneous conclusion. Traina says, "Employment of Scriptural statements without their prior evaluation may lead to spiritual disaster" (Traina, p. 204).

The Whole Bible

The Principle It is not sufficient to just meditate on a truth as it occurs in one book of the Bible. Meditation must go beyond the borders of the book in which a truth is found. Every truth gleaned from an individual book must be considered in light of every other truth related to that subject elsewhere in the Bible.

For example, Matthew 7:1 says, "Judge not that you be not judged." One might conclude that all judging is wrong in every case, but a moment's reflection would indicate that this is an erroneous conclusion. Other passages command believers to judge. First Corinthians 6:2 says, "Do you not know that the saints will judge the world? And if the world will be judged by you, are you unworthy to judge the smallest matters?" Paul goes on in that passage to argue forcefully that the Corinthians should be judging some things in their assembly. After considering both passages, the only possible conclusion is that there are things we are not to judge, but, on the other hand, there are things we must judge.

A Caution In a sense, this phase of meditation is like doing a mini-topical study. Other passages in that particular biblical book or other books of the Bible on the same subject are being considered. In thinking about the same subject in several books of the Bible, the context of each passage must be kept in mind. Certainly, before drawing final "formal" conclusions, a study of these other passages must be conducted in context.

Obviously, immature or less knowledgeable believers will not be able to handle a subject in the Bible like someone more familiar with the total sweep of Scripture. That should not be surprising. The same thing is true in any field, such as law, medicine, mechanics, etc.

Beyond the Bible

Hirsch makes some distinctions. According to him, understanding is an individual's personal "perception" (my word, not his) of the meaning of the text. Explanation is the explaining of the meaning of the text to others. Application is applying the meaning of the text "to me, to us, to our particular situation." It is the use or value of the text. He adds that interpretation includes both understanding (an individual understands the meaning of the text), and explanation (an interpreter explains the text to others). Understanding is the personal side of interpretation and explanation is the public side of interpretation. Moreover, interpretation sometimes includes explanation and application, such as a Sunday morning sermon (Hirsch, 1976, p. 19). These distinctions are commonly understood.

Hirsch also makes a distinction that is not always realized. He says there is a difference between meaning and significance. Meaning is the whole meaning of the text and significance is the meaning of the text in relation to a larger context, that is, another mind, another subject, another era, a system of values, etc. (Hirsch, 1976, pp. 2-3). This is a helpful distinction.

Johnson agrees with Hirsch that the application of a passage of Scripture is different than the significance of the passage. Application refers to relating the author's message to the believer. It is the climactic aspect of interpretation. Significance involves evaluation in which the message of the text is weighed and integrated into a personal worldview. It is not a part of textual interpretation (Johnson, p. 238).

In thinking through what the Bible says, consideration should be given to the significance of what is said beyond the Bible itself. It is the larger context of ideas. For example, what is the significance of Genesis 1 in relation to evolution?

Summary: Part of meditating on God's Word is evaluating any given truth in light of its immediate context, the context of the book, the context of the Bible as a whole, and even the context of ideas beyond the Bible.

Another word for this phase of meditation could be correlation. The ultimate aim of all Bible study is to correlate all the truth in the Bible on any given subject, issuing in a systematic statement of that truth. That's precisely what systematic theology attempts to do with specific major themes in the Scripture.

Traina states: "*Always correlate.* One should constantly look for connections between biblical passages, Scriptural statements, and the data one finds outside the Scriptures. *One should constantly attempt to see the Bible as-a-whole and life as-a-whole*" (Traina, p. 226, italics his).

In the 1950s, Unger wrote, "Meditation upon God's Word is fast becoming a lost art among many Christian people. This holy exercise of pondering over the Word, chewing it as an animal chews its cud to get its sweetness and nutritive virtue into the heart and life takes time, which ill fits into the speed of our modern age. Today most Christians' devotions are too hurried, their lives too rushed." Unger adds, "But holiness and hurry never did suit well together. Prayer and preoccupation have always been strange bed-fellows. A head knowledge of the Word may perhaps be consonant with the scurry of the age, but not a deep heart experience of its preciousness. A deep knowledge of spiritual things can only come through unhurried reflection upon God's truth and prayer" (Unger, p. 41). If that was true, then, how much more is that true today?

This chapter has discussed meditating on the truth of Scripture in the light of the Bible. The next will discuss meditation in light of life.

Chapter **14**

MEDITATING ON THE APPLICATION OF TRUTH

Meditation can be divided into two major parts: 1) thinking through the Scripture and 2) thinking through life. The first is called evaluation or correlation and the second is called application. Armed with the truth, gleaned from contextual study and correlated with the book in which it is found as well as the whole Bible, believers are now ready to give serious thought to how that truth is applied to their life. This is meditation in the sense of application.

Actually, the object of a Bible study is application. Hirsch Jr. says the ultimate aim of interpretation is "to form a reliable basis for application." He goes on to say that the value of knowledge is in its application. Even fiction is valuable because it presents something that is not fiction. The value of fiction depends upon its human truth. The truth found in literature is not usually found in other modes of discourse. It is truth about "human nature and emotions, about the form of human desires, and the forms of resistance to human desires" (Hirsch, Jr., 1976, pp. 156-157). If that is true of all literature, how much more true is it of the Word of truth given by the God of truth?

Careful thought needs to be given to applying the truth of Scripture. What exactly should be applied? How should it be applied? Some jump too quickly from observation to an application without thinking through all the ramifications involved. The following guidelines will enable believers to think through how to apply the truths of Scripture to their lives.

Some of God's spiritual truths are stated in sentence form. Other concepts are developed over several statements or over several paragraphs, etc., of material.

Think About Commands

Historical Fulfillment Before applying any command in Scripture, make sure it is for us today. Some of the commands in the Bible are addressed to people in historical situations and were fulfilled by them at that time. They were not meant to be directly applied to anyone else.

For example, Paul told Timothy, "Be diligent to come to me quickly" (2 Tim. 4:9). That command was fulfilled historically in Timothy and is neither normative nor universal for believers today. There may be a principle involved, but Timothy fulfilled the precise commandment of Paul to Timothy. In Matthew 10, Jesus sent out the Apostles. He told them such things as, "Do not go into the way of the Gentiles, and do not enter a city of the Samaritans. But go rather to the lost sheep of the house of Israel" (Mt. 10:5-6). That passage does not apply to any situation today. It did not even apply to them for very long. Later, Jesus told them to go to the whole world (Mt. 28:19-20).

Universal Application Asked, "What is normative? What is universal?" The universal truths of the Bible are rooted in God and His relationship to people or to the relationship between people. "For I am the LORD your God. You shall therefore consecrate yourselves, and you shall be holy; for I am holy. Neither shall you defile yourselves with any creeping thing that creeps on the earth" (Lev 11:44). "As He who called you is holy, you also be holy in all your conduct, because it is written, 'Be holy, for I am holy'" (1 Pet. 1:15-16). "In this is love, not that we loved God, but that He loved us and sent His Son to be the propitiation for our sins. Beloved, if God so loved us, we also ought to love one another" (1 Jn. 4:10-11).

Many commands can and should be applied. For example, Colossians 3:18-4:1 addresses individuals. Wives are told to submit to their own husbands (Col. 3:18). Husbands are exhorted to love their wives (Col. 3:19). Children are commanded to obey their parents (Col. 3:20), etc. Each of these admonitions needs to be applied to life. It is a simple task to think about how to apply the appropriate command in your case.

Think about the Overall Principle

Concepts Most Christians are conditioned to think in terms of "verses." They memorize verses, interpret verses, and, thus, apply verses. There is nothing wrong with that. As we have just seen, that is a legitimate approach to Scripture. The problem in doing that is that it is sometimes forgotten that some spiritual truth is not taught in a single statement but is the result of the development of a thought throughout a series of statements. The concepts of Scripture gleaned from a study of sentences, paragraphs, groups of paragraphs, sections, and even divisions of Scripture need to be applied.

The unit analysis approach to the Scripture concluded that the truth of the unit should be stated or summarized in one sentence. That truth (message) should also be thought through as to how it applies to life.

An Illustration In Colossians 3:18-4:1, Paul discusses various relationships. In the process, he repeatedly refers to the Lord. Wives are to submit "as is fitting in the Lord" (Col. 3:18). Children are to obey "for this is well-pleasing to the Lord" (Col. 3:20). Servants are to obey "fearing God" (Col. 3:22) and are to do all things "heartily, as to the Lord and not to men" (Col. 3:23). Masters are to do what is just "knowing that you also have a Master in heaven" (Col. 4:1).

There is a sense in which these verses as a unit are teaching that Jesus Christ is the key to all human relationships. As we put Him in the middle of relationships and relate to others as unto Him, we will be doing what God desires of us. That concept certainly fits the theme of Colossians, which is that Jesus Christ should have preeminence in everything. So, although Colossians 3:18-4:1 does not say in any one particular verse, "relate to everyone in your life as unto the Lord," the truth of the whole passage most assuredly is teaching just that.

Think in Specifics

The Principle Paul told Timothy, "All Scripture is given by inspiration of God, and is profitable for doctrine, for reproof, for correction, for instruction in righteousness, that the man of God may be complete, thoroughly equipped for every good work" (2 Tim. 3:16-17). These verses indicate that all Scripture is God-breathed and is profitable.

The profit of Scripture is in four areas: doctrine, reproof, correction, and instruction in righteousness. Two of these four items are positive and the other two are negative. In other words, the Scripture is profitable in that it teaches some things ought not to be done and that other things ought to be done. Therefore, every believer should ask two questions of every passage: 1) What is this passage telling me I ought to take out of my life? 2) What is this passage telling me I ought to be putting in my life? This is a helpful way to apply the Word. Find specific things that either need to be added to or deleted from your life.

Illustrations In some passages, this is easy. The specifics are given in the passage. In Colossians 3:5-14, Paul specifically says to put off things such as covetousness and lying and to put on things such as humility and patience.

Most of the time, the Bible is not so specific; it speaks in general principles. For example, Colossians 3:19 says, "Husbands love your wives," but specifically, what does a husband do to apply that truth to his life? It is conceivable that one husband trying to love his wife may help her wash dishes while another husband may conclude that the loving thing to do is not help his wife with the dishes. Perhaps the husband should ask his wife what she thinks is loving. So, think about how to specifically apply the truths in a passage.

Then, sometimes, the truth is not given as directly as even a general statement; it is given indirectly. Instead of stating the truth specifically, God tells a story. From the story, we must determine the spiritual truths or principles and apply them to our lives.

One of the major problems of application is the nature of the way truth is taught in the Bible. As we have just seen, sometimes it is stated explicitly, as in the case of covetousness or humility. On other occasions, truth is generally stated, such as, "Husbands, love your wives." To assist you in determining how to specifically apply a truth to your life, you might ask exactly how others have done this. That question could be asked of people in the Bible as well as people in your life.

Aristotle said, "Generalities are the refuge of a weak mind."

Think in Terms of Every Area of Your Life

Once you have thought through the truth down to the specifics of how to implement that truth in your life, you need to think in terms of every area of your life. One of the easy and tragic mistakes believers tend to make in applying the truth of Scripture is that they apply it to one area of their life and neglect others.

The problem is we do not think. We are like the teacher when the electricity went off. He quickly moved all the students to another room. As they changed rooms, they were all buzzing, "What are we going to do? There is no electricity." The teacher, overhearing the clamor, said, "We are going to this room because there is a projector in it. We are going to see a film." He was thinking about one area—lights. The lights went out and he thought, "No problem—we'll show a film. You do not need lights for that." He applied the principle of "no electricity" to lights. He forgot you have to have electricity to run a projector!

A believer sitting in church listening to a sermon decides he needs to apply the truth of being patient to his life at work. The week before the sermon, he was impatient with a fellow employee, so in the middle of the Sunday sermon, he decided that he would be patient with that individual the next week. Sure enough, by God's grace, he is able to practice more patience toward that hateful and hostile employee than he was ever able to do before. Then, he marches home to continue being impatient with his wife and/or children!

To prevent isolated application and to ensure that the truth of Scripture permeates every area of your life, ask yourself these questions.

How do I apply this at home? Be specific. How do I apply this to my husband or wife? How does this affect my relationship with my children? Does this have anything to say about how I handle my time, my hobbies, my money, etc.?

How do I apply this at work? Again, be specific. How does this truth relate to those above me, those beside me, and those below me? What actions and attitudes need to be taken?

How do I apply this at church? Most believers put on their best behavior when they go to church. Though we look like we are applying the Scripture at church, we need to ask, "Are we really bringing the Scriptures to bear in every situation, even at church? How does this truth affect how we treat people in the parking lot? How does it affect how we treat the person who took your 'saved seat?' How does this truth determine how we make decisions in the committee or board meetings?"

Probe Possible Implications

There is one other area of application that is worthy of meditation. It can be fun as well as fruitful. Ask what the implications of this truth are. The implications of the truth of a passage of Scripture may go beyond the immediate circumstances of the historical situation of the time, but an implication of a passage must not be contrary to the passage.

Gains Ask yourself, "What will happen if I do this?" "What is gained?" "How will I benefit?" List the three, five, or ten benefits of practicing a particular truth.

Losses Ask, "What will happen if I do not do this?" "What is lost?" "How will I and others suffer?" Again, make an extensive list of all the consequences of not practicing a particular truth. Or you might ask, "Why do people not do this?" "What hinders them from practicing God's truth?" Then, create an answer for each hindrance.

Summary: It is apparent from the Scripture that God puts a premium on believers meditating on His Word. Meditation needs to be concerned about how the truth of a passage fits the rest of Scripture, and beyond that, it needs to concentrate on how believers implement the truth in their personal lives.

Scripture was not written so that scholars could write dull treatises or so that preachers could preach boring sermons. Scripture was written for life. Not until we understand Scripture in the context of current life have we done what God intended for us to do with His Word. Yet, we must not haphazardly attempt to apply Scripture without forethought. That's where meditation comes in. We must carefully consider exactly how to apply Scripture to our lives and respond to it, which is what the next section of this book will deal with in detail.

PART IV

RESPONDING TO SPIRITUAL TRUTH

Chapter **15**

THE DANGER OF BIBLE STUDY

Proceed with caution! You are on a dangerous road.

Thus far, you have traveled a long way down the road toward spiritual truth that will set you apart unto the Lord. If you have followed the path mapped out, properly prepared yourself, searched and studied, and thought long and hard about how the truth you have found fits Scripture and your life, now you must respond.

You have no choice. You will respond. It is the nature of truth. As Dr. Howard Hendricks, my former seminary professor, reminded us in his Bible study class, "Revelation demands response." The danger is that you will not respond correctly and will, therefore, end up deceived!

One of the major passages of the Bible on implementing the Word of God into your life is James 1:21-25. That passage warns all who hear the Word to beware of the danger of deception. Consider what James has to say.

Receive the Word

Put off Sin James begins by saying, "Therefore, lay aside all filthiness and overflow of wickedness, and receive with meekness the implanted word, which is able to save your souls" (Jas. 1:21). The Greek word translated "laying aside" means to "put off." It was used of putting off a garment. James says, put off your sin like you would take off your coat. He uses two words to refer to sin: 1) filthiness and 2) overflow of wickedness. The Greek word rendered filthiness was used of a dirty, badly soiled garment. Here, it is used figuratively of moral defilement. The Greek term "wickedness" can either mean "badness" or "malice." In the New Testament, it often means malice, which is probably the meaning here. These and other sins must be put off to receive the Word. Peter taught something similar (1 Pet. 2:1-3; see Part I, "Preparing for Truth").

Receive the Word After putting off sin, one is to receive the implanted Word. The implanted Word is the Word planted in believers after the new birth.

This implanted Word is to be received with meekness. The Greek word translated "meekness" was used of a wild horse that had been tamed and was now under the control of a bit and bridle. Such a horse is not weak; he is meek. His strength is under control. Thus, meekness is strength under restraint. Receiving the Word with meekness is accepting what it says and submitting to God's control. It is receiving what God has to say with a teachable spirit willing to obey.

Saving Your Life James says that for a believer to receive the implanted Word with a teachable spirit results in the saving of the soul. What does that mean? The saving of a soul is a cliche that today is used of a sinner being saved from hell, but James is not talking about sinners going to heaven. He is talking to believers. In verse 19, he addresses the readers as "my beloved brethren." He is talking to people who have had the Word planted within them (Jas. 1:21). What is the meaning of believers saving their souls?

In the first place, the word "saved" in the Bible does not always refer to being saved from hell. The word saved simply means to be delivered. It occurs five times in the book of James and in none of the five places does it refer to being delivered from damnation. For example, James speaks of prayer saving the sick (Jas. 5:15). Therefore, in James, "saved" refers to being delivered from damage, disease, and/or death. Moreover, the word "soul" means "life." In other words, James is teaching that if believers receive the Word that has been planted within them with a teachable, obedient spirit, it will save their lives from the damage of sin.

Do the Word

Believers must not only receive the Word with a teachable spirit, they must do what the word says. James adds, "But be doers of the word, and not hearers only, deceiving yourselves" (Jas. 1:22). In the next several verses, James gives two reasons why one should do what the Word says.

Not Being Deceived For one thing, if believers only hear the Word and do not do what it says, they will end up deceived. James explains, "For if anyone is a hearer of the word and not a doer, he is like a man observing his natural face in a mirror; for he observes himself, goes away, and immediately forgets what kind of man he was" (Jas. 1:23-24). In the Greek text, the word "man" means "male." If a male looks in a mirror, sees a problem and does not correct it, he will soon forget it when he walks away. Until this day, men are more likely to do that than women.

One Saturday morning, I looked in the mirror and thought, "I need to shave, but it is Saturday. I'll do it later." I soon became involved in something else and forgot that I had not shaved. It was not until late in the day that somebody reminded me that I looked like I had just gotten out of bed, that I remembered that I had not shaved.

The danger of Bible study is that believers will look into the mirror of the Word, see a problem and not do anything about it. The tendency is to forget that the problem exists. The ultimate result can be deception. Believers can think they are in good shape when they actually have a problem. They are deceived.

Being Blessed The second reason a believer should obey the Word is: "But he who looks into the perfect law of liberty and continues in it, and is not a forgetful hearer but a doer of the work, this one will be blessed in what he does" (Jas. 1:25). In short, the doer of the Word is blessed by God.

According to James, before believers can do the Word, they must "look" into it. The Greek word translated "look" in this verse is not a mere glance; it means to "stoop and look." The idea is to bend over something to get a closer look at it. It is more than reading. It is searching and studying the Scriptures. This is the type of activity discussed in Part II, "Understanding the Truth."

Next, James says believers must "continue" in the Word. This is not the normal Greek word for continue in the New Testament. This particular word means "to continue beside." The picture seems to be of camping beside the Word in contemplation. In other words, this is probably a reference to meditation, the kind of activity described in Part III.

Finally, James speaks of the believer not being "a forgetful hearer, but a doer of the work." What work does he have in mind? In verse 25, he spoke of looking into "the perfect law of liberty." The perfect law of liberty is the law of love. In chapter 2, James says believers will be judged by the law of liberty (Jas. 2:12), which in that passage includes showing mercy (Jas. 2:13). The law of liberty is the law of love. So doing the work of the Word is the labor of love.

The believer who obeys the Word of God, particularly the law of love, is blessed by God (Jas. 1:25). In the context of James 1, the blessing of God consists of things like maturity (Jas. 1:4), completeness (Jas. 1:4), wisdom (Jas. 1:5), a crown of life (Jas. 1:12), and practical righteousness (Jas. 1:20).

Summary: Believers who receive the Word with a teachable spirit will save their lives from the damage of sin, and God will bless them. The danger is that believers will hear, not heed what God says, and end up deceived.

Beware. Do not take the road of deception. Make sure you do what God says.

In his commentary on Revelation, Barclay says, "The devout student is the best of all students. There are too many who are devout but not students. They will not accept the discipline of study and of learning, and they even look with suspicion upon the further knowledge that study brings to men. There are equally too many who are students but not devout. They are interested too much in intellectual knowledge and too little in the life of prayer and in the life of service of their fellowmen. A man would do well to aim at being not only a student, and not only devout but at being a devout student" (Barclay, *Revelation*, vol. 2, p. 286).

Chapter 16

THE APPROPRIATE RESPONSE

A young girl who thought of herself as a pre-adult decided to play a mother in the kitchen. She dreamed of baking a cake just like Mom, but unlike Mom, she decided to do it her way. She felt no particular need to follow the exact directions in the cookbook. Needless to say, the resultant cake was not too tasty.

It is possible to attempt to do what God says, but do it your way. The result will not be the spiritual maturity that He promised. Therefore, we must respond properly to the recipe for living found in the Scripture. What are the essential ingredients of an appropriate response?

Response is to God

Not to Rules One of the occupational hazards of handling the Bible is reducing it to rules and, thus, becoming legalistic. The all-time geniuses at this were the Pharisees of old. There is a little Phariseeism in all of us. Legalism kicks the heart out of biblical Christianity. Who wants to live by rules? Something is limiting and restricting about that. We much more readily respond to a person than principles.

To God The right response to biblical truth is not to rules and regulations. It is not even to principles and precepts. The appropriate response is to God Himself.

God commissioned Jonah to preach to the ancient city of Nineveh. When he finally got around to doing that, the text states, "Then he cried out and said, 'Yet forty days and Nineveh will be overthrown!'" (Jonah 3:4). Obviously, there was more to his message. That one brief sentence is simply the summary statement of what he had to say. Surely, he told them that God expected them to turn to Him and trust Him. The question is, what was the response of the Ninevites?

The text of Jonah 3 says, "So the people of Nineveh believed God" (Jonah 3:5). That is an interesting statement. Jonah preached. The expected response would have been that the people of Nineveh believed Jonah. Obviously, they did, but beyond that, their response was not just to Jonah but to God.

We as believers must learn to read the Bible as a personal letter from God and respond to Him and not just to it. If we think of what the Scripture says as a rule or regulation, we will tend to want to violate it, but when our response is to Him, we will much more readily bow to the precepts of His Word.

The chief of police wants you to obey the speed limit. One way he attempts to get that done is to post speed limit signs along the streets, but just because we see speed limit signs does not mean we obey the speed limit. On the other hand, imagine the chief of police being your personal friend and sitting in the front seat of your car as you drive. Responding to him personally would be vastly different than responding to the speed limit signs. You would tend to keep the speed limit because of his presence. In a similar fashion, we must remember that our right response is not just to the Word of God posted in the Bible, it is to the God of the

Word. That kind of response produces internal godliness, not just external conformity.

Response is Motivated by Love

Without Love In emphatic and eloquent terms, Paul declares that without love, an individual is nothing and all of his activities profit him nothing. "Though I speak with the tongues of men and angels, but have not love, I am become as sounding brass and a clanging cymbal. And though I have the gift of prophecy, and understand all mysteries and all knowledge, and though I have all faith, so that I could remove mountains, but have not love, I am nothing. And though I bestow all my goods to feed the poor, and though I give my body to be burned, and have not love, it profits me nothing" (1 Cor. 13:1-3). To obey the Bible because "you have to" is not what God wants. To do what the Bible says because other people are watching you is to miss the point.

With Love We respond to God because He loves us. John wrote, "We love Him because He first loved us" (1 Jn. 4:19). God wants us to do what He says, but He wants us to do it from the heart. He says, "If you love Me, keep My commandments" (Jn. 14:15). When we respond to Him because we love Him, we are properly responding to God.

If a response without love profits me nothing, a response with love profits everything. The profit is both now and later. Paul told Timothy, "For bodily exercise profits a little, but godliness is profitable in all things, having promise of the life that now is and that which is to come" (1 Tim. 4:8).

Response is to Trust and Obey

Believe Him The Bible repeatedly declares that the proper response to God is faith.

- "But without faith, it is impossible to please Him, for he who comes to God must believe that He is, and that He is a rewarder of those who diligently seek Him" (Heb. 11:6).
- "I have been crucified with Christ; it is no longer I who live, but Christ lives in me; and the life which I now live in the flesh I live by faith in the Son of God, who loved me and gave Himself for me" (Gal. 2:20).
- "For I am not ashamed of the gospel of Christ, for it is the power of God to salvation for everyone who believes, for the Jew first and also for the Greek. For in it the righteousness of God is revealed from faith to faith; as it is written, the just shall live by faith" (Rom. 1:16-17).
- "That Christ might dwell in your hearts through faith" (Eph. 3:17).

Faith is believing and trusting. God wants believers to believe what He says.

Trust Him Faith is also trusting God for the enablement to do what He says. As believers depend on the grace of God, they have the power of God to obey the Word of God.

Obey Him Faith produces love, obedience, praise, patience, etc. When we believe what God says and trust Him for the grace to do what He says, we lovingly, willingly, and readily obey Him. The issue in obedience is faith.

The Appropriate Response

Suppose your house was on fire and you wanted everyone to evacuate. If you screamed at the top of your lungs, "The house is on fire!" whether or not they obeyed and evacuated the premises would be dependent on whether or not they believed your statement. If they believed you, they would obey you.

On the other hand, unbelief produces disobedience. Parents and pastors look at disobedient children and church members and wish they could get them to obey. Perhaps they ought to ask themselves, "How can I get those individuals to believe?" It is when people believe that they obey. It is when they do not believe that they disobey.

Thus, to know the truth of the Bible, believers must respond to it with faith and obedience. Johnson says, "But without a faith-obedience response, there is no true understanding, nor is there complete knowledge that follows upon response to the truth of God (1 Cor. 2:14-16). Such theoretical knowledge is inadequate when dealing with God's self-revelation. At this point of moral and spiritual response, the Spirit-empowered person can truly understand and in time gains a fuller knowledge of the truth" (Johnson, p. 108).

Rick Warren says, "God does not owe you an explanation or reason for everything He asks you to do. Understanding can wait, but obedience cannot. Instant obedience will teach you more about God than a lifetime of Bible discussions. In fact, you will never understand some of His commands until you obey them first. Obedience unlocks understanding" (Warren, *The Purpose Driven Life*, p. 72).

In his commentary on the Gospel of Luke, Wiersbe observes, "There are so many 'Bible studies' these days (and many of them are helpful) that you wonder if a student can learn anything from a simple text in the Bible. We must not despise Christian scholarship but also keep things in balance." Later, he adds, "As helpful and necessary as theological studies are, the most important requirements for Bible study are a yielded heart and obedient will" (Wiersbe, *Be Compassionate*, pp. 131-132).

If you are to know the Word, you must believe it, trust the Lord, and obey it. A Chinese student told his teacher he was having intellectual tensions studying biblical criticism. He added, "I have found new light in the Holy Scriptures since I began reading and behaving it!" (Kuist, p. 60). To know the Word, you must behave it.

Response Results in Knowledge of God

Jesus Studying the Bible results in knowledge of the Bible. Appropriate response to God through His Word results in knowledge of God. When we respond by faith to God in love, we end up knowing God. That's what Jesus promised the disciples in the upper room. He told them: "At that day, you will know that I am in my Father, and you in Me, and I in you. He who has My commandments and keeps them, it is he who loves Me. And he who loves Me will be loved by my Father, and I will love him and manifest Myself to him" (Jn. 14:20-21).

Paul Paul echoed the same truth, "For this reason, we also, since the day we heard of it, do not cease to pray for you and to ask that you may be filled with the knowledge of His will in all wisdom and spiritual understanding; that you may have a walk worthy of the Lord, fully pleasing Him, being fruitful in every good work and increasing in the knowledge of God; strengthened with all might, according to His glorious power, for all patience and long-suffering with joy; giving thanks to the Father who has qualified us to be partakers of the inheritance of the saints in the light" (Col. 1:9-12).

Paul asks that believers be "filled with the knowledge of His will" (Col. 1:9), which comes from being filled with the knowledge of God's Word. The result or consequence of being filled with the knowledge of God's will is that believers will walk worthy of Him, pleasing Him (Col. 1:10). Beginning at this point in the passage, Paul itemizes some of the elements that constitute a life-pleasing to the Lord. In the Greek text, these are expressed by four participles rendered in English by 1) "being fruitful" (Col. 1:10), 2) "increasing in the knowledge of God" (Col. 1:10), 3) "strengthened with all might" (Col. 1:11), 4), "giving thanks" (Col. 1:12). In other words, one of the results of being filled with the knowledge of God's will, which comes from His Word and walking worthy of Him, is that we will increase in our knowledge of Him. As believers respond to the Word of God with faith and love, they get to know the God of the Word.

Summary: Believers are to respond by faith to God in love to get to know Him. The Bible was not written to inform us but to transform us. Thus, truth studied must be truth applied.

It is possible to study the Bible and only know the Bible. That's an abortion of the God-intended process. God did not breathe His Word onto pages for doctrinal formation alone, but for character formation.

How To Study The Bible

To study the Bible just to know the Bible is like studying the frame of a picture instead of the painting or staring at the window frame instead of the sea outside the window. Donald Grey Barnhouse told about staying in a room overlooking the Atlantic Ocean. He imagined writing a letter to a friend who had never seen the sea. His imaginary letter said, "We have a beautiful room with a picture window that gives us a sweeping view of the ocean. The window is twelve feet two inches long and four feet eight inches high. It is divided into three sections. We have taken a scraping of the glass and have had it analyzed and can tell you the chemical formula of the glass. We have had an expert from one of the great glass companies tell us all about the glass and we are giving you a history of the invention and development of glass.

"The glass is set in steel frames that are painted black. We have had the steel and the paint analyzed and you can read the analysis in our second and third studies affixed to this letter. We have discovered that the panes of glass are kept in the frames by a putty composition. We have scraped down some of this putty and are giving you a long addendum on its chemical composition.

"Finally, we have inquired of the hotel management and found out their method of keeping the windows clean. You will be delighted to know from the subjoined study the whole process of the window-cleaning and the formula of the special detergent needed to cope with the salt spray from the ocean. In closing, let us say that we hope you have enjoyed our study of the ocean."

Barnhouse added, "We smile at such a fanciful parable. It must be admitted that there are people who can name for you the books of the Bible, give you the history of the Jewish people, list the kings of Judah and Israel along with a mass of background material about the written Word of God, but who seem to forget that the Bible exists only to bring us to the Lord Jesus Christ. He is the ocean beyond the window. The young man might decide that seeing the ocean was not worth the trip to the Atlantic Coast. If it were no more than a study of the window through which the ocean might be seen, he would be right (Donald Gray Barnhouse, *Romans*, vol. IV, pp. 87-88).

The Bible was not written to be an end in itself. It was written that we may know God. "When you are sick, you want a doctor and not a medical book or a formula. When you are being sued, you want a lawyer and not a law book. Likewise, when you face your last enemy, death, you want the Saviour and not a doctrine written in a book" (Wiersbe, *Be Alive*, p. 137).

Mary Lathbury wrote:

> Break now the bread of life, dear Lord, to me,
> As thou didst break the loaves beside the sea,
> Beyond the sacred page, I seek Thee Lord,
> My spirit pants for Thee, Oh living Word.

PART V

SHARING SPIRITUAL TRUTH

Chapter 17

BEGIN AT HOME

God never intended to give anyone truth and have it stop with that person. God always gives His Word to someone so that individual would give it to someone else. That was the case in the Old Testament. God gave His Word to Israel so they would give it to the world. It was also true in the New Testament. He gave His truth to believers so they would broadcast it to the whole world.

Therefore, part of Bible study is Bible sharing. If you receive truth and do not distribute truth, you will only produce deadness, but when you receive truth and you become the channel for it to be given to others, it will in the process, produce life in you. The Dead Sea is dead because it is the lowest spot on the face of the earth. Water comes into it, but does not flow out of it. Hence, there is no life. To absorb truth, we must give it away.

Share the Scripture with Your Mate

The place to begin sharing the truth of Scripture is at home. The husband is commanded to teach his wife the Word of God. Paul wrote, "Husbands, love your wives, just as Christ loved the church and gave Himself for it, that He might sanctify and cleanse it with the washing of the water by the Word, that He might present it to Himself a glorious church not having spot or wrinkle or any such thing, but that it should be holy and without blemish" (Eph. 5:25-27).

In these verses, Paul is saying that a husband is to love his wife. A careful consideration of what follows indicates that He means that a husband is to meet the wife's spiritual needs. In verse 26, Paul says this is done "by the Word." An implication, if not the explanation of this passage, is that a husband is to share the Word of God with his wife. So much so is that true that Paul said in 1 Corinthians 14:35 that if a wife had questions, she was not to ask them at church, at least in the public assembly, but was to go home and ask her husband.

Though the Scripture does not specifically mention a wife teaching her husband the Scripture, it is appropriate for a wife to share what she has learned from the Word with her husband. Some women possess the gift of teaching and older women are instructed to teach younger women (Titus 2:4). Aquila and Priscilla, a husband and wife, corrected and instructed Apollos in the things of the Lord (Acts 18:26). If they shared the Scripture together with Apollos, surely they shared the Scripture with each other.

Share the Scripture with Your Children

Moses, the author of the first five books of the Bible, told us what we should do with the Word of God. He said: "And these words which I command you today shall be in your heart. You shall teach them diligently to your children, and shall talk of them when you sit in your house, when you walk by the way, when you lie down, and when you rise up" (Deut. 6:6-7).

Moses insisted that the Word of God be "in your heart." Then, he instructed parents to diligently teach their children. Believers are to first appropriately respond to God themselves. Then, they are to share that Word with their family. When the God-ordained procedure is followed, the ones sharing the Word become an example to their family.

Deuteronomy 6 does not suggest that parents erect a pulpit in the living room and preach to their children. Instead, they are to teach their children by talking about the Word of God throughout the day, from when they get up in the morning until when they lie down at night. They are to share the Scripture when they sit and walk (Deut. 6:7). You should share the Word of God with your family at mealtime, bedtime, and anytime you are with them. It should be as natural to talk about the Lord and His Word as it is to sleep, eat, and walk.

The New Testament specifically points to the father as the one who is to teach his children the Word of God. Paul says, "And you, fathers, do not provoke your children to wrath, but bring them up in the training and admonition of the Lord" (Eph. 6:4). The fact that this verse is addressed to fathers does not necessarily mean that mothers are not to teach their children. They are responsible too. It does mean, however, that fathers are to be involved in the process and, perhaps, implies that they are ultimately responsible.

Summary: God gives us His truth so that we can pass it on to others, beginning with our families.

God never intended for us to know the truth and preach it before we practice it. We must practice it first; it will naturally flow out of our being. As Henry David Thoreau said, "A man must see before he can say … at first brush, a man is not capable of reporting truth. To do that, he must be drenched and saturated with it. Then the truth will exhale from him naturally."

Likewise, to teach the truth to others before you have taught it to your family is an abortion of the God-designed process. If we follow God's plan, we will have more godly leaders in our churches and fewer failures among them.

Chapter **18**

LET THE WHOLE WORLD KNOW

When I find a "good deal" like a super sale on men's clothes, I tell my family and friends. Frankly, that's fun! They benefit, get excited, and share the good news with their friends. Occasionally, I've told a merchant, "You owe me a commission!" To date, none have taken me seriously.

God gave His truth to us so we could be set apart to Him and so we would give it to others for them to share in a relationship with Him as well. As important as it is to begin at home, we dare not stop there. God desires that the whole world know Him and His truth. So let the whole world know, beginning with your world.

At Church

Many passages teach that every believer is responsible for sharing spiritual truth with other believers, especially in the context of the assembly. The writer to the Hebrews admonished, "Not forsaking the assembly of ourselves together as is the manner of some, but exhorting one another, and so much the more as we see the day approaching" (Heb. 10:25). Paul told the Colossians, "Let the word of Christ dwell in you richly in all wisdom, teaching and admonishing one another in psalms and hymns and spiritual songs, singing with grace in your hearts to the Lord" (Col. 3:16). He told the Thessalonians, "Therefore, comfort each other and edify one another, just as you also are doing" (1 Thess. 5:11). The very purpose for equipping saints is "for the work of the ministry" (Eph. 4:12).

At Work

Technically, the Scripture does not mention our lives "at work" in the modern sense of the term. However, several passages in the New Testament speak directly to slaves. The principles in those passages certainly apply to the modern work situation. For example, Paul told slaves to "adorn the doctrine of God, our Savior, in all things" (Titus 2:9). As they obeyed God's truth, they shared truth with others throughout their lives.

While demonstrating the truth of God with one's life is essential, proclaiming God's truth is the essence of sharing. Without words, works could be misunderstood. Without words, there is no clear message. For others to know who is responsible for your conduct, at some point, they have to hear you say you're doing it for Jesus Christ. So the truth must be shared through your lips as well as your life.

Thus, at work, we should take off the morally dirty coat of the old life (Jas. 1:21) and put on the new coat of the teachings of God's Word (Titus 2:9). We need to wear the right clothes and speak the right words at work.

To the World

Unfortunately, most of the ministry of the Word is limited to home, church, and possibly work. God wants us to share His Word with the whole world. We are to share the gospel with all those who are lost (Mk. 16:15) and we are to teach them "to observe all things" that Jesus Christ has commanded (Mt. 28:20).

How you spread the Word to the world depends on your resources and spiritual gift. All believers should do all they can to spread the Word to the whole world. You can use your resources to support men and women around the world who are teaching the Word of God.

You can use your gift to do it as well. If you have a speaking gift, why not use that ability as much as you can to teach the principles of the Word of God? If you have a serving gift, use that gift to support ministries that accurately and effectively spread God's truth throughout the world.

Putting the truth that God has taught you on paper and distributing that paper to others is another form of sharing. Had the authors of Scripture not done that, we would have no Bible! This kind of sharing could be more permanent than your speech or steps. God communicated the truth to us in written form. We should take the clue from Him and do likewise.

Summary: We can share the truth God has taught us through our lives, with our lips, through literature, text, email, social media, and even film.

Believers are to share the Word of God by their walk and talk to their family and fellow believers and, beyond that, to the whole world. Bible study is incomplete until the truth we have discovered is shared with others.

I sincerely doubt that you will ever know the truth of the Word of God until you have experienced it and taught it several times.

CONCLUSION

Simply put, the sum is that God wrote a book filled with spiritual truth so that believers could be set apart to Him and share His truth with others. Admittedly, mining the ore of spiritual truth is sometimes difficult and time-consuming, but maturity is not easy, nor does it take place overnight. However, the end product is worth the work.

If you have concluded that the procedure presented in this book is too time-consuming, I would like to make a suggestion. Take, however, much time you have to study and systematically apply this approach until you have made it through one book of the Bible. If you only have one hour a week and methodically study for a year, you would have mastered at least one biblical book and probably more at the end of that year. After several years of using this method, you will know more about the Scripture than you would otherwise.

There is an ancient and anonymous prayer that applies to all who would study the Bible for themselves, "From the cowardice that shrinks from new truth, from laziness that is content with half-truths, from arrogance that thinks it knows all truths, Oh God of truth, deliver us."

My prayer is that you will be a brave, diligent, humble seeker of God's truth and that when you find it you will not be content until you have practiced it and shared it with as many people as possible. May you be like Ezra, who "prepared his heart to seek the Law of the Lord, and to do it, and to teach statutes and ordinances in Israel" (Ezra 7:10).

> Seek the truth
> Listen for the truth
> Teach the truth
> Love the truth
> Abide in the truth
> And defend the truth unto death.
>> John Hus,
>> Czech reformer, born 1373
>> Burned at the stake 1415

APPENDIX I

WHICH TRANSLATION IS BEST FOR BIBLE STUDY?

To evaluate which translation is best for Bible study, one must understand two issues: theories of which Hebrew and Greek text is closest to the original and theories of which translation philosophy is the most accurate.

Theories of the Hebrew and Greek Texts

The Old Testament was written in Hebrew, with several small portions in Aramaic and the New Testament in Greek. The original manuscripts no longer exist. Copies do exist. The question is, which of these copies is closest to the original?

Old Testament The Jews meticulously copied the Hebrew (and Aramaic) Old Testament. They did things like counting each letter on a page, copying the page, and counting the letters on the copy to make sure that they had the correct number. As a result, we no doubt have a very reliable copy of the original today.

Before the discovery of the Dead Sea Scrolls, the oldest copy of the Hebrew Old Testament was the Masoretic Text, dated about AD 900. A copy of Isaiah, dated about 200 BC, was found in the discovery of the Dead Sea Scrolls. In other words, with the discovery of the Isaiah scroll, we jumped 1100 years closer to when the original Hebrew manuscripts were written. The differences between the Isaiah of the Dead Sea Scrolls and the Isaiah of the Masoretic Text are few and minor. In a few places, there are differences concerning things like the presence or absence of an article and the differences between a singular and a plural. That's incredible! There is little doubt that we have an accurate copy of the Hebrew Old Testament.

There are, however, some problems. In some places, the text in the Old Testament is obscure. On occasion, there is a word that appears only once in all of the Old Testament. Other versions of the Old Testament exist. The Samaritans have a version of the Pentateuch, which differs from the Masoretic Text in some places. There was also a Greek translation of the Old Testament, called the Septuagint (a.k.a. the LXX), done about 250 BC.

Some modern English translations closely follow the Masoretic Text, while others practice revision, altering the Masoretic Text based on the Septuagint, etc.

The New Testament Unfortunately, the care taken with the Old Testament Hebrew text was not taken with the New Testament Greek text. Consequently, there are many more differences in the existing New Testament manuscripts than in the Hebrew Old Testament. Here is what happened.

From the time of the writing of the New Testament until the invention of the printing press, Christians had to copy the New Testament by hand. Many of these handwritten documents still exist today. There are better than 6,000 manuscripts (handwritten copies) of the New Testament. Some of these manuscripts contain the whole New Testament, and others contain only portions of the New Testament.

Appendix 1

Johann Gutenberg invented the printing press with movable type about 1450. The first major product of Gutenberg's press was a Bible, Jerome's Latin Vulgate. In 1488, a Hebrew Old Testament was printed. The first printed Greek text of the New Testament was published on March 1, 1516. Erasmus, a Catholic priest who taught at Cambridge University from 1509 to 1514, edited six manuscripts of the Greek New Testament to produce the first printed Greek text of the New Testament.

Erasmus' work has been severely criticized. It is only based on a few manuscripts of the Greek New Testament. His single manuscript on the Book of Revelation did not contain the last six verses. So Erasmus translated the Latin Vulgate version of these verses into Greek. Between 1516 and 1535, Erasmus published five editions of the Greek text of the New Testament (the third edition of 1522 included 1 John 5:7, which had been omitted in the first two editions).

Robert Stephanus produced four editions of the Greek New Testament in 1545, 1549, 1550, and 1551. Stephanus' third and fourth editions agreed very closely with the fourth and fifth editions of Erasmus, which were gaining wide acceptance as the text of the New Testament. Stephanus' third edition was the first time the text was divided into numbered verses.

Theodore Beza, the successor of Calvin at Geneva, produced ten editions of the Greek New Testament. Nine were published during his lifetime and one after his death (only four were independent editions, those of 1565, 1582, 1588-89, 1598). Beza's text rarely departed from the fourth edition of Stephanus (one nineteenth-century scholar said that Beza's text only differed in 38 places from the fourth edition of

Stephanus).

The King James Version relied mainly on the later editions of Beza's Greek text (1588, 1598), which was very close to the editions of Erasmus and Stephanus.

In 1624, Bonaventure and Abraham Elzevir, Dutch printers in the city of Liden, published their first edition of the New Testament. The text followed Beza's editions but included readings from Erasmus and others. In the second edition, published in 1633, the phrase *Textus Receptus* first appeared: "You have therefore the text now received by all in which we give nothing changed or corrupt."

If there were only handwritten manuscripts in basic agreement and one printed Greek text, there would be no problem and no confusion. The plot thickens! In the nineteenth century, other manuscripts began to appear and, eventually, an entirely different edition of the Greek text was printed.

In 1859, Tischendorf discovered a manuscript in St. Catherine's monastery on Mt. Sinai. It was appropriately named Codex Sinaiticus. This manuscript predated any other manuscript known at the time. There was another manuscript. In the Vatican was a manuscript appropriately named Codex Vaticanus. Some considered these two manuscripts to be the earliest manuscripts of the New Testament.

In 1881, two English scholars, Westcott and Hort, printed a Greek text of the New Testament based mainly on Vaticanus and Sinaiticus. Other Greek texts followed, including the Nestle Text and the Greek New Testament, published by the United Bible Society. These Greek texts follow Codex Sinaiticus, Codex Vaticanus, as well as a few manuscripts, and are essentially the same.

Appendix 1

Thus, today, there are over 6,000 manuscripts (handwritten copies) and several Greek texts (printed editions) of the New Testament. There are two theories as to which Greek text is closest to the original: the traditional/majority type of Greek text (the *Textus Receptus*) and what is called the eclectic or critical Greek text (the Westcott and Hort text, the Nestle Text, or United Bible Society text).

The King James Version and the *New King James Version* are based on the traditional/majority type of Greek text. All other modern English translations of the Bible are based on an eclectic Greek text, primarily dependent upon Sinaiticus and Vaticanus.

When I was in college, I was introduced to this textual problem of the New Testament and after some study on my own, I opted for the eclectic textual theory. I even defended the theory in a debate. As a seminary student, I heard nothing that changed my mind. When I graduated from seminary, I was a convinced textual critic and, for several years after that, practiced textual criticism in my study of the Scriptures.

Then, inadvertently, I discovered some things I did not know. I'd always thought all the reasonable evidence was on the side of the eclectic Greek text. To my surprise, I discovered that there was not only a reasonable but a strong case to be made for the traditional/majority type of text. For six months, I did nothing but read material, pro and con, on the theory I rejected as a college student. Eventually, I concluded that I was wrong and became convinced that the traditional/majority text type better represented the autographs of the New Testament. The reasons I switched to the majority text type are technical and complicated, but briefly, they amount to this:

1. The traditional/majority text type comes from the area where almost all of the autographs were originally written or where they were sent and, therefore, were first copied, including the Gospel of John, 1 and 2 Corinthians, Galatians, Ephesians, Philippians, Colossians, 1 Timothy, Titus, Philemon, 1 and 2 Peter, 1 John, and Revelation.

2. The vast majority of all manuscripts support the traditional/majority type of text. Eighty to ninety percent of all Greek manuscripts are in such agreement that they comprise a family of manuscripts. This family of manuscripts has been called by various names: the Syrian text, the Byzantine text, the *Textus Receptus*, the traditional text, and the majority text.

Erasmus was criticized for only using six manuscripts of the New Testament. The reality is that if any six manuscripts were selected out of a majority of manuscripts, the result would be virtually the same type of text.

How does one explain the fact that the vast majority of manuscripts support the traditional/majority? Westcott and Hort explained this away by concluding that this text type was a late redaction of the existing manuscripts about 400 years after Christ. They went so far as to insist that a man named Lucian did the work, but there is no evidence in church history that such an official redaction ever took place. Later theories claim that the majority text type evolved slowly over a long period of time. Is not a better explanation that this text type was closer to the original and, therefore, there was more time to produce more copies?

3. There is unity within the traditional/majority text family.

Appendix 1

There is remarkable unity within the traditional/majority text type of manuscripts. In fact, most Greek manuscripts display more uniformity than the Vulgate, an official fourth-century edition of the Latin manuscripts by Jerome. That's incredible! The majority of Greek manuscripts consist of smooth Greek text with no grammatical, historical, or geographical errors. The other Greek manuscripts, namely Sinaiticus and Vaticanus, do not have such uniformity and contain numerous mistakes.

4. The traditional/majority type text has been used throughout the centuries. Until recently, the church has used the majority-type text of the New Testament. It was used hundreds of years before the Protestant Reformation. It was the text of the Protestant Reformation and the text used during the revivals and modern missions movement since the Reformation. Is it not impressive that throughout history, until the latter part of the nineteenth century, the church used the traditional/majority type of Greek text?

Did God hide the "best manuscripts" on the back shelf of the Vatican (Vaticanus) and in St. Catherine's monastery on Mt. Sinai (Sinaiticus) until 1881? Are we to believe those two manuscripts are the best because they predate the majority by a few years? It is significant that both Sinaiticus and Vaticanus have numerous mistakes in them and differ widely from the majority and each other.

Did God preserve His Word through the centuries? If He did, the traditional/majority text type must be closer to the original because it was the one preserved. This argument will not appeal to everyone. It will only appeal to people who believe in the inspiration and the preservation of the Word of God, but as one Greek professor said, "To what better kind of a person would you want to appeal?"

Theories of Translation

The task of the translator is to communicate the content of a written text into another language. The goal is to translate what the original author wrote accurately. There are two different theories as to how accuracy is best accomplished.

The "complete equivalence" theory (also called "literal" or "formal equivalence") points out that written material consists of words and structure. Therefore, an accurate translation should correspond as closely as possible to the elements of the original, word for word, phrase for phrase, clause for clause, and sentence for sentence. In other words, it should have "linguistic equivalence."

The "dynamic equivalence" theory (also called "idiomatic" and "impact") claims the issue of accuracy is determined by the response of the reader of the translation. Their concern is for the correspondence of thought and ideas—"equivalence of effect." Thus, there are basically two philosophies of translation.

Complete Equivalence	Dynamic Equivalence
Formal Literal	Dynamic Idiomatic Impact

Since no two languages are identical in the meaning of corresponding words or structures, there can be no absolute, literal translation. No formal equivalence translation of the Bible can preserve the precise grammatical structure of the original Hebrew and Greek texts. Accommodations must be made in English structure for clear communication. A pure literal translation of the Bible would read like an interlinear! On the other hand, all dynamic equivalence-translations must have at least some formal equivalence to the original; otherwise, it would not qualify as a translation at all.

Thus, every translation of the Scripture is a mixture of formal equivalence and dynamic equivalence, but that does not mean that the differences in translation are differences in the degree of formal or dynamic equivalence. While it is true that no translation is completely literal or completely dynamic, each translation is produced with one or the other theories in mind. The difference is one of kind, not degree.

There is a sense in which the dynamic equivalence theory of translation has a legitimate point. Translators certainly do not want to be so slavishly tied to the structure of the original that they produce something in English that is awkward and does not communicate what the original author intended. However, there is a danger. The tendency and temptation of dynamic equivalence is in the name of "equivalent effect" to explain too much. Once translators unnecessarily depart from the original structure, they begin to interpret instead of translate.

Granted, word order must be changed to produce an intelligent English sentence. When such changes are necessary, they should be done. The problem is that once translators adopt the dynamic equivalence theory, they almost always make changes that are not necessary. Should not sentences in the original be translated as sentences? If the original author wrote complex sentences, should not complex sentences appear in the translation? If the original author was ambiguous, should not the translation reflect that? Does the translator have the right to omit important words, such as conjunctions, which are clues to meaning? Must the translator eliminate technical terms? If the translators add words, should they not alert the reader to that fact by putting the additional words in italics?

The issue is, "Should translators practice dynamic equivalence to the point that they make unnecessary changes?" Ideally, the translator should give the reader what the original author said and the way he said it, at least as much as possible. What is needed is a translation that is as complete and equivalent as possible in every sense of the word.

Summary: When determining which English translation to use for serious Bible study, the two major issues are the greek text type and the translation theory.

Well, what translation is best for Bible study? Assuming that the student needs a translation based on most New Testament manuscripts and one that uses a complete equivalent translation theory, the New King James Version is the best translation in modern English for Bible study. If the student prefers an eclectic Greek text, the best translation for Bible study would be the New American Standard Bible. The New International Version should be avoided for the type of Bible study recommended in this book. It often omits structural data that is essential to determining the structure and meaning of the text.

APPENDIX II

AN OUTLINE OF BIBLE HISTORY

Origins (Genesis 1-11) Earth, Man, Sin, Present State, Language

I. Patriarchs (Genesis 12-50) 2167-1860 BC

    A. Abraham
    B. Isaac
    C. Jacob

II. Exodus (Exodus-Deuteronomy) 1527-1407 BC

    A. In Egypt
    B. In Wilderness
    C. At Sinai
    D. In Wanderings
    E. In Plain of Moab

III. Conquest (Joshua) 1407-1390 BC

    A. Conquest
    B. Dividing
    C. Charge

IV. Judges (Judges-1 Samuel 8) 1390-1043 BC

    A. Deborah
    B. Gideon
    C. Samson

V. United Kingdom (1 Samuel 9-1 Kings 11, Chron., 2 Chron. 1-9) 1043-931 BC

    A. Saul
    B. David
    C. Solomon

VI. Divided Kingdom (1 Kings 12-2 Kings 16, 2 Chron. 10-36) 931-722 BC, 606 BC

    A. Northern Kingdom
    B. Southern Kingdom

VII. Captivity (2 Kings 17-25) 606-536 BC

    A. Northern Kingdom
    B. Southern Kingdom

VIII. Restoration (Ezra-Esther) 536-400 BC

    A. Zerubbabel
    B. Ezra
    C. Nehemiah

IX. Ministry of Christ (Matthew-John) 6 BC-30 AD

    A. Preparation
    B. Ministry
    C. Suffering
    D. Triumph

X. Acts of the Apostles (Acts) 30-95 AD

    A. Jerusalem
    B. Judea and Samaria
    C. Uttermost parts

APPENDIX III

THE USE AND ABUSE OF COMMENTARIES

Some sincere saints believe the only tool for Bible study is the Bible. They disdain the use of other tools, such as commentaries. They argue: "I have the Holy Spirit. He teaches me. I do not need commentaries." Uneducated believers who live in undeveloped areas of the world have been known to claim that, and so have highly educated seminary graduates who feel that since they know Greek and Hebrew, they need no other outside help. Even purists who practice inductive Bible study might argue that they do not need commentaries. They study the Scripture firsthand for themselves. Commentaries to them are a crutch for the lazy.

How does one justify the use of commentaries? A biblical answer is simple. God has s given gifted teachers to the church. If it is legitimate to learn from a gifted teacher, it is legitimate to learn from commentaries, for a commentary is nothing more than a teacher's writing. The question is not, "Should we or should not," but "Why?" "Which ones?" and "How?".

Why use Commentaries?

Linguistic Information One of the major reasons for using a commentary is to obtain linguistic information one cannot know otherwise. If the student does not know Greek or Hebrew at all, a commentary can supply grammatical and syntactical information and insight. Even the meaning of words can be helpful.

For example, in John 21, Jesus said to Peter, "Do you love me more than these?" Peter replied, "You know I love you" (Jn. 21:15). There is no way an unaided English reader would know that two different Greek words for love are being used. A good commentary would explain the meanings of the original words.

Even those who know Greek and Hebrew can find helpful linguistic information in commentaries. No one knows it all. So, commentaries can be helpful to everyone in the area of linguistic data.

Social Customs The Bible was written thousands of years ago in a different land where people practiced many different social customs than today. Sometimes, these customs are apparent. They are so different that we immediately recognize them as some social or legal custom. A good commentary would explain the custom.

Many customs in the Bible are easy to miss. In John 19, Pontius Pilate offered to free a criminal instead of Christ. The reader has no way of knowing that it was the custom of the day for the governor to free a criminal during Passover, unless the reader was aware of John 18:39. Pilate was attempting to get out of his dilemma by utilizing that custom. Commentaries are helpful in that they explain customs the reader might have missed.

Observations There is more, much more. Commentaries can assist students of the Word by noting observations they did not make. Needless to say, a passage has many more observations than any student will ever make. A good commentator will make observations in the passage that even a careful student missed.

Implications Commentators will teach students implications they did not know. For example, James 5 says that believers are to confess their faults to one another. The uninformed reader of that passage would not know that the Roman Catholic Church uses that passage to teach the confession of sins to a priest. Is that implication valid? Many would say, "No," because the passage says the sins are to be confessed to "one another," which is a reciprocal pronoun meaning that two parties are to confess to each other. Therefore, if this passage teaches the confession of sins to a priest, it also teaches priests to confess their sins to believers. Commentaries will often explain such implications of the biblical text.

Which Commentaries should be Used?

Every Christian home should have a study Bible. I recommend *The NKJV study Bible* (I wrote some of the notes in that study Bible) and *The Ryrie Study Bible*. I have written a commentary on every book of the Bible, free at *insightsfromtheword.com*. I would highly recommend "Dr. Constable's Expository (Bible Study) Notes." His commentary on every book of the Bible is free at https://planobiblechapel.org/constable-notes/. Other commentaries I recommend include *The Bible Knowledge Commentary* (Edited by John F. Walvoord and Roy B. Zuck. Wheaton: Scripture Press Publications, Victor Books), *The Bible Believer's Commentary* by William MacDonald (edited by Arthur Farstad, Nashville: Thomas Nelson Publishers, 1989), and *Be* series by Warren Wiersbe. More advanced students will find help in the Tyndale

Series and the New International Commentary Series.

There are three kinds of commentaries—exegetical, expositional, and devotional. Exegetical commentaries deal with the original language and the text of Scripture in a detailed fashion. This kind of commentary is usually technical, especially concerning grammar. An expositional commentary explains the English text. The author may or may not know Hebrew and Greek, but he or she does not discuss the original languages in the commentary. Devotional commentaries are more applicational than expositional. All three types of commentaries are helpful.

How to Use Commentaries

Commentaries should be used in the same way that two porcupines love each other, carefully. The key to using commentaries is to remember that the Bible was written at different times in different cultures using different types of literature and languages. Therefore, Bible students have to study history, culture, literature, and language. That observation is the clue as to how to use commentaries.

For example, when reading commentaries, look for historical data. Do not just look for the author's opinions. Look for historical data, including cultural background and customs. See if they comment on the type of literature being utilized and the implications for the meaning within the passage. Notice linguistic information, including syntactical data and the meaning of words.

Of course, many commentators skip the history and language information and just give their interpretation. That certainly has

Appendix 3

its place. At the same time, let the student beware. The commentator's interpretation may not be correct. Donald Grey Barnhouse began his exposition of Romans 5:19 with the words, "I would be disobedient to the Holy Spirit if I accepted the explanation of this text which most commentators had given." So, as you read commentaries, ask yourself some questions. Does the commentator prove his interpretation? Does the commentator give you his conclusions, or does he prove his conclusions? The best support for any interpretation is, first and foremost, contextual support followed by linguistic data, the type of literature, and the historical background. Is the author prejudiced? Before using any commentary, find out as much as possible about the author. What is his point of view? What are his prejudices? His predisposition to a doctrinal position may heavily influence his interpretation of a passage.

Summary: Commentaries are both proper and productive if used properly. The comments of godly men can confirm and correct our own observations.

Perhaps the greatest drawback of using commentaries is that they are so focused on the technical data that they often miss the message of the passage. Mickelsen writes, "Both liberal and conservative scholars give their minds so strenuously to authorship, sources, and backgrounds that they had a little energy left to spend on the message and what it means (A. Berkeley Mickelsen, "The New Hermeneutics," p. 6). In his commentary on Romans, Karl Barth complained that scholars have often buried themselves in textual problems so deeply that they never heard the message Paul was preaching.

Spurgeon once observed, "Two opposite errors beset the student of the Scriptures: the tendency to take everything secondhand from others and the refusal to take anything from others." Traina strikes a balance when he says, "When a reasonable amount of time has been devoted to it (independent study), then the interpreter should investigate secondary sources" (Traina, p. 163).

BIBLIOGRAPHY

Barclay, William. *The Revelation of John.* Philadelphia: The Westminster Press, vol. 2.

Bair, Deirdre. *Jung.* Boston: Little, Brown and Company, 2003.

Barnhouse, Donald Grey. *God's Covenants, God's Discipline, God's Glory.* Grand Rapids: Wm. B. Eerdmans Publishing Company, June 1983, Vol. IV.

Boonstra, Harry. "Biblical Metaphor—MoreThan Decoration," *Christianity Today,* December 17, 1976.

Bultmann, Rudolph. *Jesus Christ and Mythology.* New York: Scribner's, 1958.

Cooper, David, L. *Future Events Revealed.* Los Angeles: Biblical Research Society, 1935, revised in 1983.

Dana, H. E., and Mantey, Julius R. *A Manual Grammar of the Greek New Testament.* New York: The Macmillan Company, 1927.

Foster, Richard, J. *Celebration of Discipline.* San Francisco: Harper SanFranciso, 1988.

Gray, James M. *How to Master the English Bible.* Chicago: Moody Press, 1951.

Hadjiantoniou, G. A. *The Postman of Patmos.* Grand Rapids: Zondervan Publishing House, 1961.

Hirsch, Jr., E. D. *The Aims of Interpretation.* Chicago and London: The University of Chicago Press, 1976.

_____ *Validity in Interpretation.* New Haven and London: Yale University Press, 1967.

Johnson, Elliott E. *Expository Hermeneutics: An Introduction.* Grand Rapids: Zondervan Publishing House, 1990.

Jensen, Irving L. *Independent Bible Study.* Chicago: Moody Press, 1963.

Kaiser, Jr., Walter. *Toward An Exegetical Theology*. Grand Rapids: Baker Book House, 1981.

Kuist, Howard Tissman. *These Words Upon Thy Heart*. Richmond: John Knox Press, 1947.

Longman III, Tremper, "Reading the Bible like a Book," *Christianity Today*, March 6, 1987.

Robinson, Haddon W. *Biblical Preaching*. Grand Rapids: Baker Book House, 1980.

Rudolph, Erwin P. "*Beauty in the Bible*," *Christianity Today*, December 5, 1975.

Ryken, Leland. *The Literature of the Bible*. Grand Rapids: Zondervan Publishing House, 1974.

Schodde, George Henry. "*Interpretation*" in *ISBE*, BiblesoftElectronic Database, 1996.

Tan, Paul Lee. *The Interpretation of Prophecy*. Winona Lake, IN: BMH Books, 1976.

Terry, Milton. *Biblical Hermeneutics*. Grand Rapids: Zondervan Publishing House.

Torrey, R. A. *How to Study the Bible for Greatest Profit*. New York, Chicago, Toronto: Fleming H. Revell Company, 1896.

Traina, Robert A. *Methodical Bible Study*. New York: The Biblical Seminary, 1952.

Unger, Merrill F. *Pathways to Power*. Grand Rapids: Zondervan Publishing House, 1953.

Wagner, Don M. *The Expository Method of G. Campbell Morgan*. Westwood, N.J.: Revell, 1957.

Wald, Oletta. *The Joy of Discovery*. Minneapolis: Bible Banner Press, 1956.

Warren, Richard and Shell, William A. *Dynamic Bible Study Methods*. Wheaton: Victor Books, 1981.

Westcott, B. F. *The Gospel According to John*. London: James Clarke, 1958.

Wiersbe, Warren W. "Prokope," Vol. III, No. 2, March-April 1986.

_____ *Be Alive*. Wheaton: Victor Books, 1986.

_____ *Be Compassionate*. Wheaton: Victor Books, 1989.

About The Author

G. Michael Cocoris is a gifted communicator. He can make even complicated subjects simple, clear, and practical. His breadth of experience has allowed him to relate to a wide range of audiences.

Michael received a Bachelor of Arts degree from Tennessee Temple University, a Master of Theology degree from Dallas Seminary, and a Doctorate of Divinity from Biola University. He traveled the United States for over a dozen years as a speaker. He has also been a seminary professor, visiting lecturer, and world traveler, including hosting tours to Israel and China.

Michael has pastored three churches, including a rural church when he was in seminary, an urban church, the historic Church of the Open Door, first in downtown Los Angeles and later in Glendora, California, and a suburban church, the Lindley Church in Tarzana California, a suburb of Los Angeles. While at the Church of Open Door, he had a daily radio broadcast.

Michael has written numerous magazine articles, mainly for *Biblical Research Monthly*. He has authored a number of books, including *Seventy Years on Hope Street, A History of the Church of the Open Door*; *The Spiritual Life, Clarifying the Confusion; Repentance, The Most Misunderstood Word in the Bible; Evangelism: A Biblical Approach; The Salvation Controversy; Lordship Salvation: Is It Biblical?; The Books of the Bible, the Subject, Structure, Situation, and Significant Verses of Each Book; Psalms, A Song for Every Situation, Each Summarized on One Page; and Counseling Theories: A Simple Explanation and Biblical Evaluation*. In addition, he was a contributor to The *NKJV Study Bible* and *Nelson's New Illustrated Bible Commentary*.

Michael is the pastor of the Lindley Church in Tarzana, California. He and his wife, Patricia, live in Santa Monica, California.

www.ingramcontent.com/pod-product-compliance
Lightning Source LLC
Chambersburg PA
CBHW070051080526
44586CB00013B/1012